On the MOVE

Refresher Course

Course Book

**von
Shauna Payne**

D1665989

Ernst Klett Sprachen
Barcelona · Budapest · London · Posen
Sofia · Stuttgart

Refresher Course

von
Shauna Payne

Practice Sections
Chris Bye

Beratung
Sibyl Marquardt,
Fachbereichsleiterin Englisch
an der Volkshochschule Reutlingen

1. Auflage 1 4 3 2 | 06 05 04 03

Alle Drucke dieser Auflage können im
Unterricht nebeneinander benutzt werden,
sie sind untereinander unverändert.
Die letzte Zahl bezeichnet das Jahr dieses
Druckes.
© Ernst Klett Sprachen GmbH,
  Stuttgart 2003.
Alle Rechte vorbehalten.
Internetadresse: http://www.klett-verlag.de

Redaktion: Edda Vorrath-Wiesenthal
              Nicola Tuson
Gestaltung: Achim Hutt

Einbandgestaltung: Christine Schneyer
Illustrationen: Sepp Buchegger,
                  Beate Klauder
Umschlagfoto: Courtesy of PIER 39,
                  San Francisco
Reproduktion: Meyle + Müller,
                  Medien-Management,
                  Pforzheim.
Druck: H. Stürtz AG, Würzburg
ISBN 3-12-524129-4

Introduction

Sie haben schon einmal Englisch gelernt und wollen Ihre verschütteten Kenntnisse auffrischen und vertiefen? Dann seien Sie herzlich willkommen beim *On the MOVE Refresher Course*, dem Auffrischkurs für alle, die praktisches Englisch auf Reisen, am Arbeitsplatz oder ganz einfach als unentbehrliches internationales Kommunikationsmittel in der Welt von heute benötigen.

In 16 Lektionen **(Units)** wiederholen Sie zügig die wichtigsten Grammatikthemen, reaktivieren und erweitern Ihren Wortschatz und lernen, sich in alltäglichen Situationen auf Englisch wieder zurechtzufinden.

Mit dem Schnelltest **(Quick Quiz)** am Ende jeder Lektion können Sie die wichtigsten Inhalte jeweils wiederholen und bei Bedarf die entsprechenden Abschnitte in der Lektion noch einmal nachschlagen.

In der **Practice Section**, die Sie im Anschluss an jede Lektion finden, haben Sie Gelegenheit zum ausführlichen Üben des Lernstoffes im Selbststudium.

Die Wiederholungslektionen **(Revision Units)** 4, 8, 12 und 16 bieten die Möglichkeit, durch zusätzliche Aktivitäten im Unterricht wichtige Inhalte der vorangegangenen drei Lektionen spielerisch anzuwenden und damit Ihr Wissen zu festigen.

Im Anhang befinden sich eine Grammatikübersicht **(Grammar Overview)**, die Lösungen **(Keys)** zu den *Practice Sections* und sämtliche Hörtexte **(Tapescripts)**. Ein lektionsbegleitendes Wörterverzeichnis **(Unit Vocabulary)**, in dem die neuen Wörter in der Folge ihres Erscheinens aufgelistet sind, sowie ein alphabetisches Wortregister **(Alphabetical Word List)** schließen den Anhang ab.

Mit der zum Kurs gehörenden Kassette / CD können Sie zu Hause oder unterwegs die Hörtexte noch einmal anhören.

Last but not least finden Sie einige nützliche Redewendungen für die Verständigung im Unterricht auf der Innenseite des vorderen Buchdeckels und auf der Innenseite des hinteren Buchdeckels die wichtigsten Zahlen und Zeitangaben.

Und jetzt wünschen wir Ihnen viel Spaß und Erfolg mit dem *On the MOVE Refresher Course!*

- ◆ **Refresher Course Book**
  ISBN 3-12-524129-4
- ◆ **1 Kassette zum Course Book**
  ISBN 3-12-524133-2
- ◆ **1 CD zum Course Book**
  ISBN 3-12-524134-0
- ◆ **Teacher's Book**
  ISBN 3-12-524131-6

Contents

Contents

Hören

Zu Schritten mit diesem Symbol gibt es einen Hörtext. Mit Hilfe der Kassette / CD können Sie das Hörverstehen üben, Ihre Aussprache trainieren oder die Lösung einer schriftlichen Aufgabe überprüfen.

Lesen

An diesem Symbol erkennen Sie Lesetexte zu interessanten landeskundlichen oder interkulturellen Themen aus der englischsprachigen Welt. Zu diesen Texten gibt es keine spezielle Aufgabenstellung, so dass sie sich besonders gut zum Lesen zu Hause eignen.

Information

In den grünen Kästen mit dem i-Punkt werden Zusatzinformationen zu Grammatik oder Wortbedeutung gegeben. In den *Practice Sections* enthalten sie darüber hinaus auf Deutsch kurze Erläuterungen zu sprachlichen Besonderheiten.

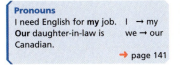

Pronouns
I need English for **my** job. I → my
Our daughter-in-law is we → our
Canadian.
→ page 141

Grammatik

In den blauen Kästen werden die wichtigsten Grammatikinhalte hervorgehoben. Jeder Kasten enthält jeweils das Grammatikthema als Überschrift, einen Beispielsatz sowie den Verweis auf die entsprechende Seite in der Grammatikübersicht. In den *Practice Sections* finden Sie darin außerdem deutsche Grammatikerläuterungen.

Getting to know each other

1 **I need English for ...**

A **Write the sentences under the pictures.**

66 I work for a travel agency. 99

66 I often show customers around our production department. 99

66 We love travelling. 99

66 Our daughter-in-law is Canadian. 99

66 I'm unemployed at the moment. 99

B **Complete the texts. Then listen and check.**

> live   English   travel   important   speak   job
>
> can   at the moment   countries

1. I need English for my _____ . I often show customers around our production department. Sometimes there are groups from other countries, so I need to explain everything in _____ .

2. I work for a travel agency. I travel a lot in my job. I often go and look at hotels in Finland and other European _____ and English is spoken everywhere.

3. Our daughter-in-law is Canadian, and our grandchildren _____ English. They _____ in Canada. We want to visit them in the summer.

4. I'm unemployed _____ . English is very _____ for me because all companies want people who can speak English.

5. We love travelling, and we _____ abroad a lot. When you speak English you _____ go everywhere.

> **Pronouns**
> I need English for **my** job.   I → my
> **Our** daughter-in-law is Canadian.   we → our
>   → page 141

C **Why are you learning English? Complete the form.**

First name: _____

Surname: _____

I need English

☐ for my job.

☐ for travelling.

	Yes	No
My friends / family speak/s English.	☐	☐
I often travel abroad.	☐	☐

Other reasons: _____

_____

_____

_____

_____

D **Now introduce yourself to the class.**

My name's ....

I need English ...

2 Word collection

A **What things do you have with you? Label them in English.**

B Collect them. How many are there?

There are four pens, two dictionaries, …

There's one mobile phone.

1	2	3	4	5	6	7	8	9	10
one	two	three	four	five	six	seven	eight	nine	ten

Mr, Mrs, Miss or Ms?

In English-speaking countries people often only use first names. But what do you do if you only have someone's surname?
Ms is neutral and is used more and more often for both married and single women.
Mrs is only for married women.
Miss is only used for young single women.
Mr is only for men.

3 Saying hello and goodbye

Listen and complete the dialogue.

see you	I'm fine	You too	you	to meet	thanks
way	too	how are you	Hello	have	

■ Hi!

▲ _____!

■ How are _____?

▲ Not so bad, _____ and, _____?

■ _____, thank you.

▲ By the _____, this is Nicole. She's from Jena. She needs English for her job.

■ Hello, Nicole, nice _____ you.

● Hello, nice to meet you, _____.

■ Well, _____ a nice evening.

▲ Thank you. _____.

■ See you next week.

▲ OK, _____. Bye.

■ Goodbye.

she → her
he → his

Present Simple
She needs English for her job.
➜ page 137

Pronunciation. Listen and practise.

1. Hi. How are you?
2. Not so bad, thanks.
3. Nice to meet you.

4. Nice to meet you, too.
5. Have a nice evening.
6. Thank you.

7. See you next week.
8. Goodbye.

C **Introduce each other.**

Hello. How are you?

Nice to meet you.

By the way, this is Nicole.

The verb *to be*
I'**m** fine.   **am**
How **are** you?   **are**
She'**s** from Jena. **is**
➜ page 137

Quick Quiz

Grammar

Complete the sentences with verbs from the units.

1. There _____ groups from other countries.

2. I _____ a lot in my job.

3. Our grandchildren _____ English.

4. They _____ in Canada.

5. I _____ unemployed at the moment.

6. English _____ very important for me.

7. We _____ travelling.

8. She _____ English for her job.

Vocabulary

Match the pronouns with the possessive pronouns.

| her | its | their | your | ~~my~~ | your | our | his |

I _my_____   we _____

you _____   you _____

he _____   they _____

she _____

it _____

Phrases

Complete the phrases.

1. _____ are you?

2. I'm _____, thanks.

3. _____ the way, ...

4. _____ to meet you.

5. Have a _____ evening.

6. _____ you next week.

In Unit 1 haben Sie:
- sich und andere kurz vorgestellt.
- über Gründe zum Englischlernen gesprochen.
- gelernt, wie Sie Ihren Wortschatz erweitern können.

GRAMMATIK GRAMMATIK GRAMMA?

→ Die dritte Person (Einzahl) im Present Simple
→ Das Zeitwort *to be*
→ Besitzanzeigende Fürwörter
→ Mehrzahlformen bei Hauptwörtern

A Setzen Sie das passende besitzanzeigende Fürwort ein.

| your | our | his | my | her | their |

1. I'm Thomas. I need English for _____ job.

2. _____ name's Maria.

3. _____ name's Michael.

4. We want to visit _____ grandchildren in the summer.

5. They live in England, but _____ children live in Canada.

6. How are you? And how is _____ daughter?

B Die Mehrzahlformen der folgenden Wörter kommen alle in *Unit* 1 vor. Tragen Sie sie in die richtige Gruppe ein.

| hotel | grandchild | customer | group | dictionary | company | country | woman | name | man |

-s	-ies	irregular
_____	_____	_____
_____	_____	_____
_____	_____	_____
_____		

C Beschreiben Sie die folgende Person.

Name:	*Maria Lopez*
From:	*I'm from Barcelona, Spain.*
Hobbies:	*I love sport and travelling abroad.*
Reasons to learn English:	
	I work for a travel agency and need English for my job.

Her name's _____

She _____

_____

_____

_____

> **Present Simple**
> • In der Present Simple-Form wird bei der dritten Person (*he, she, it*) normalerweise an die Grundform des Zeitworts ein **-s** angehängt, z.B. *She need**s** English for her job.*
> • Bei allen anderen Personen (*I, you, we, you, they*) steht die Grundform des Zeitwortes, d.h. ohne ein **-s** am Ende.

D Nummerieren Sie die folgenden Sätze in der richtigen Reihenfolge.

☐ I'm fine, thanks. By the way, this is Chris.

☐ Nice to meet you, too.

☐ Thanks. You too. Goodbye.

☐ Hi! How are you?

☐ Well, have a nice evening.

☐ Bye!

☐ Hello, Chris. Nice to meet you.

☐ Not so bad, thanks. And you?

E Schreiben Sie die Aussage zu jedem Foto in die 3. Person um. Achten Sie auch auf die Fürwörter.

> I often show customers around our production department.

> I travel a lot in my job.

> Our grandchildren speak English.

> We travel abroad a lot.

> I'm unemployed at the moment.

1. *He often shows* _____.
2. _____.
3. _____
4. _____
5. _____

> **Das Verb *to be***
> Das Verb (Zeitwort) *to be* (sein) wird unregelmäßig gebildet.
> In der gesprochenen Sprache verwendet man normalerweise
> die Kurzformen: *I'm, you're, he's, she's, it's, we're, you're, they're.*

F Bilden Sie Sätze und setzen Sie dabei das Zeitwort *be* in die richtige Form.

1. I • from • Paris • be

_____.

2. be • you • how

_____?

3. moment • unemployed • be • at • he • the

_____.

4. sometimes • customers • there • other • be • countries • from

_____.

5. our • this • department • be • production

_____.

6. there • agency • travel • be • one

_____.

G Suchen Sie die folgenden Wörter im Kasten und kreisen Sie sie ein. Sie können waagerecht und senkrecht, aber auch diagonal und rückwärts geschrieben sein.

job

company

customer

people

production

surname

hotel

department

K	F	B	H	T	O	I	Z	O	I	U	O	K	N
P	G	B	G	T	N	I	Z	J	O	B	G	K	A
D	E	C	H	T	O	E	E	B	I	U	O	C	S
V	H	O	T	E	L	D	M	O	I	U	H	U	C
C	F	M	P	T	G	I	A	T	I	U	O	S	G
T	N	P	H	L	O	S	N	O	R	U	F	T	V
H	F	A	G	T	E	I	R	J	I	A	I	O	N
F	R	N	O	I	T	C	U	D	O	R	P	M	W
E	X	Y	N	T	O	I	S	D	I	U	O	E	Q
K	F	B	H	T	O	W	Z	H	I	U	O	R	D

People and countries

1 **The friendliest country in Europe?**

A **Read the text and look at the pictures. Which country is it?**

_____ is the best!

Following a survey of its readers, the British newspaper "The Guardian" reports that _____ is the most popular holiday destination. An official from the National Tourist Board explains why:

"First of all the weather is not as bad as people think. We are not just famous for snow, in the summer it is sunnier and warmer than in Britain and the days are longer, so you have more time. In _____, you can hike, cycle, play golf, or go rafting. The beaches are excellent and the water is much cleaner than most places in Europe. Accommodation is more comfortable than in Britain and there are a lot of different restaurants. Food is cheaper than in other countries and just as good, if not better! The people are very friendly, _____ is great for families. _____ is the best place for a holiday!"

Is it Norway?

Comparisons

Comparatives	**Superlatives**
warmer	friendliest
sunnier	the most popular
more comfortable than	

➜ page 143

B **Complete the table with words from the text in A.**

1 **One-syllable words**

warm	_____	warmest
long	_____	longest
clean	_____	cleanest
cheap	_____	cheapest
_____	greater	greatest

2 **Two-syllable words that end in –y**

| sunny | _____ | sunniest |
| _____ | friendlier | friendliest |

3 **Most other two-syllable words**

| _____ | more famous | most famous |

4 **Words with three or more syllables**

popular	more popular	_____
comfortable	_____	most comfortable
_____	more excellent	most excellent

5 **Exceptions**

| _____ | worse | worst |
| _____ | _____ | _____ |

C **What do the British like about their favourite holiday country? Complete.**

weather: *sunny,*_____

days: _____

beaches: _____

water: _____

accommodation: _____

food: _____

people: _____

D **Pairwork. Give three reasons why you like your favourite holiday country.**

I like Italy because the beaches are excellent.

I like England because the people are friendly.

So do I.

2 People and countries

A Which nationalities do you associate with the things in the pictures?

Dutch, Swiss _____

How do you spell "Portuguese"?

Can you write "Dutch" on the board, please?

_____

_____

B Listen and tick the nationalities you hear.

☐ Swedish	☐ German	☐ Russian	☐ Irish
☐ British	☐ Finnish	☐ Portuguese	☐ Polish
☐ Swiss	☐ European	☐ Belgian	☐ Danish
☐ Greek	☐ Dutch	☐ Austrian	☐ Spanish
☐ Italian	☐ Japanese	☐ French	☐ Norwegian

C Create a poster about your favourite country and present it to the class.

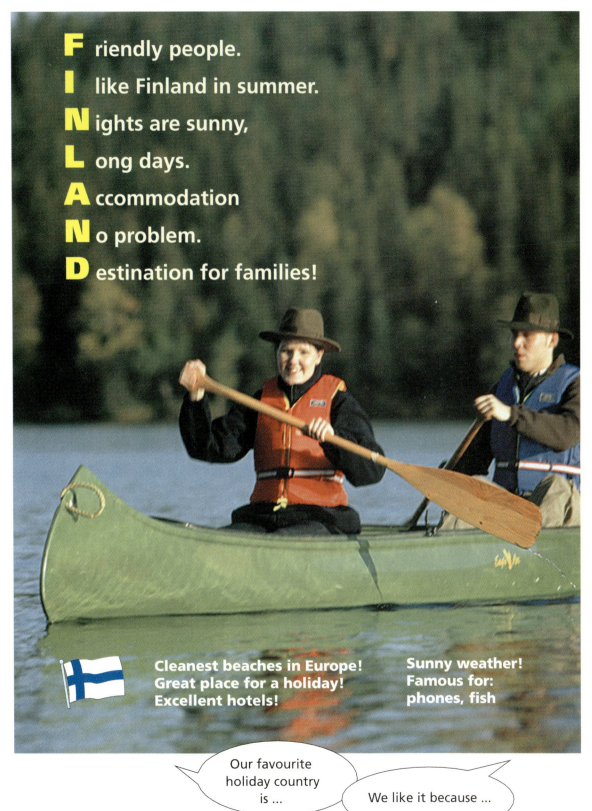

F riendly people.
I like Finland in summer.
N ights are sunny,
L ong days.
A ccommodation
N o problem.
D estination for families!

Cleanest beaches in Europe!
Great place for a holiday!
Excellent hotels!

Sunny weather!
Famous for:
phones, fish

Our favourite holiday country is ...

We like it because ...

3 I'd like to speak to ...

 A Read the beginning of a telephone conversation and listen. Tick what the caller does.

> Hello, I'd like to speak to Helen Brown, please.

> I'm afraid Helen isn't in at the moment.

☐ He calls again later. ☐ He leaves a message.

B Match the beginnings of the questions and the endings.

1. Can you ...   your telephone number?
2. How do you ...   leave a message?
3. What's ...   spell that?
4. Would you like to ... ask her to call me back?

C Now complete the telephone conversation with the questions from B.

■ Hello, I'd like to speak to Helen Brown, please.

▲ I'm afraid Helen isn't in at the moment.
_____?

■ Yes, please. _____?
My name's Rivero, Martin Rivero.

▲ Yes, of course. _____?

■ It's R – I – V – E – R – O.

▲ And _____?

■ It's 040 763 21 22.

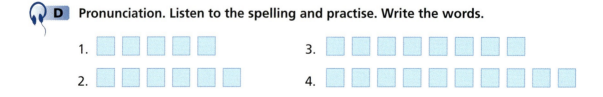 **D** Pronunciation. Listen to the spelling and practise. Write the words.

1. ☐☐☐☐☐   3. ☐☐☐☐☐☐☐

2. ☐☐☐☐☐☐   4. ☐☐☐☐☐☐☐☐☐

E Role Play. Call your partner.

Quick Quiz

Grammar

Complete the comparisons and the questions from the unit.

1. Finland is the _____ popular holiday destination.

2. The summer is *s*_____ and *w*_____ than in Britain.

3. Accommodation is more comfortable _____ in Britain.

4. Food is just ____ good _____ in other countries, if not _____.

5. _____ your telephone number?

6. _____ ____ _____ spell that?

Vocabulary

Write the nationality next to the country.

1. France _____
2. Portugal _____
3. Finland _____
4. Norway _____
5. Belgium _____
6. Switzerland _____
7. Germany _____
8. Denmark _____

Phrases

Put the phrases in order.

1. beaches • because • I • Italy • like • the • excellent • are

   _____.

2. do • I • So

   _____.

3. write • please • board, • Can • on • you • the • "Dutch"

   _____?

4. speak • please • I'd like to • Helen, • to

   _____.

5. to call me • Can • back • you • ask • her

   _____?

23

In Unit 2 haben Sie:
- über Ihre bevorzugten Urlaubsländer gesprochen.
- nach der Schreibweise von Wörtern gefragt.
- ein Telefongespräch geführt.

GRAMMATIK GRAMMATIK GRAMMAT

→ Steigerungsformen von Eigenschaftswörtern
→ Fragen

A Entziffern Sie die Eigenschaftswörter und schreiben Sie sie in die richtige Gruppe.

	einsilbig	zweisilbig	drei- oder mehrsilbig
1. xeelenctl	_____	_____	_____
2. gater	_____	_____	_____
3. ndliefry	_____	_____	_____
4. ularpop	_____	_____	_____
5. caphe	_____	_____	_____
6. dab	_____	_____	_____
7. cformtoable	_____	_____	_____
8. ancle	_____	_____	_____

Steigerung von Eigenschaftwörtern

Wie ein Eigenschaftswort gesteigert wird, hängt von der Anzahl seiner Silben ab:

- Bei einsilbigen Eigenschaftwörtern werden **-er** bzw. **-est** angehängt (*warm, warmer, warmest*).

- Endet ein zweisilbiges Eigenschaftswort auf -y, wird es zu **-ier** bzw. **-iest** (*sunny, sunn-ier, sunn-iest*). Die meisten anderen zwei- sowie alle mehrsilbigen Eigenschaftswörter werden mit **more ... than** bzw. **the most** gesteigert (*popular, more popular than, the most popular*).

- Ausnahmen zu diesen Regeln sind z.B. *good – better – best, bad – worse – worst*.

B   Setzen Sie die Eigenschaftswörter in der richtigen Form in den Text ein.

beautiful   bad   expensive   good

friendly   sunny   cheap   famous

❝I love England! I think the people are very _____.
Accommodation is sometimes more _____ than in other countries, but the bed and breakfast places are much _____ than hotels. I love them!
The food is not as _____ as people think, there are a lot of excellent restaurants. The breakfast is probably the most _____

in Europe. In countries like Italy or Spain the weather is warmer and _____ than in England, but I think the countryside is more _____ . And they have great beaches.
For me the _____ holiday country is England.❞

C Setzen Sie aus den Silben Wörter zusammen und tragen Sie sie in das Kreuzworträtsel ein. Wie lautet das Lösungswort?

aurant

be

peo

sum

ment

tion

ple

ach

rest

accom

moda

mo

mer

D Übersetzen Sie.

1. Ich möchte bitte mit Samantha Brown sprechen.

_____.

2. Ich fürchte Samantha ist im Moment nicht da.

_____.

3. Ja natürlich.

_____.

4. Mein Name ist Freud, Annabel Freud.

_____.

ℹ️ *Oh* oder *zero*?

In Großbritannien wird die Null in Telefonnummern normalerweise *oh* ausgesprochen, in Nordamerika dagegen *zero*.

Übrigens: Die Ziffern einer Telefonnummer werden im Englischen immer einzeln gegeben, z.B. 763 21 22 – *seven six three, two one, two two*. In Großbritannien werden gleiche Ziffern als z.B. *double two* gesprochen.

E **Die folgenden Fragen könnten in einem Telefongespräch sehr nützlich sein. Bringen Sie sie in die richtige Reihenfolge.**

1. please • your •? name • what's

   _____,_____?

2. do • how • that • spell • you

   _____?

3. me • him • you • to • call • can • back • ask

   _____?

4. telephone • what's • your • number

   _____?

5. message • a • leave • to • like • you • would

   _____?

6. I ? can • message • a • leave

   _____?

F **Tragen Sie die Nationalitäten zu den Ländern je nach ihrer Endung in die richtige Gruppe ein.**

Sweden   Italy   Germany   Finland   Japan

Russia   Portugal   Austria   Poland

Denmark   Spain   Norway

- ish   - ese   - an

_____   _____   _____

_____   _____   _____

_____   _____

_____   _____

_____

27

Working in Europe

1 **What do they do?**

A **Complete the sentences.**

ⓘ vet = veterinarian

flowers | in an office | chef | vet | on a farm | an engineer

1. She's a _____
   in a restaurant.

2. She's a _____.

3. They work _____.

   and / _____.

4. He works _____.

5. She sells _____.

6. He's _____.

The indefinite article
a restaurant   an office
a chef   an engineer
                 ➜ page 142

B Listen and number the activities in the order you hear them.

Picture

☐ She's playing the piano.

☐ He's looking after his children.

☐ He's working in the office.

Picture

☐ They're singing in a choir.

☐ She's learning Spanish.

☐ She's making coffee.

C Pairwork. Make a sentence for each of the pictures. Compare with a partner.

> She's a chef in a restaurant, but at the moment she's learning Spanish.

Present Simple	**Present Continuous**
She**'s** a chef in a restaurant.	At the moment she**'s** **learning** Spanish.
	➜ page 137

2   What do you always do?

A Pronunciation. Listen and practise the questions from the questionnaire.

	Yes			No
	always	usually	sometimes	never
1. Do you have breakfast at home?	☐	☐	☐	☐
2. Do you forget names?	☐	☐	☐	☐
3. Do you use English in your job?	☐	☐	☐	☐
4. Do you read a daily newspaper?	☐	☐	☐	☐
5. Do you go shopping at the weekend?	☐	☐	☐	☐
6. Do you enjoy your work?	☐	☐	☐	☐
7. Do you go on holiday in winter?	☐	☐	☐	☐

Questions
Do you **have** breakfast at home?
➜ page 137

B   Pairwork. Interview a partner with the questions in A.

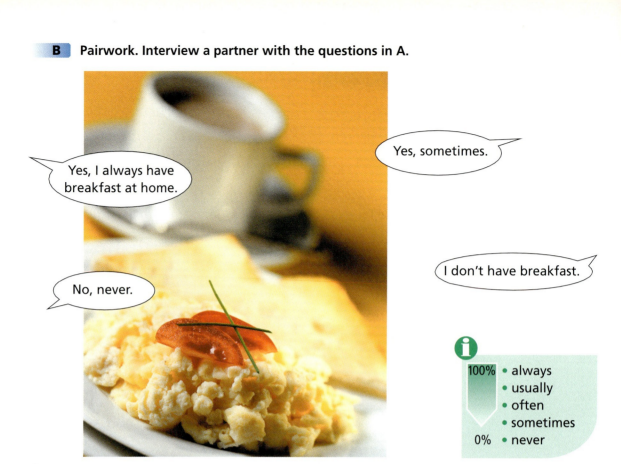

Yes, sometimes.

Yes, I always have breakfast at home.

I don't have breakfast.

No, never.

100% • always
• usually
• often
• sometimes
0% • never

Adverbs of Frequency
I **always** have breakfast at home.
→ page 143

C   Tell the group something about your partner.

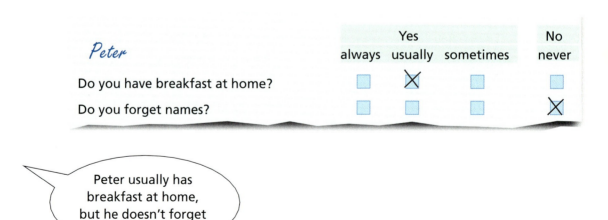

Peter	Yes			No
	always	usually	sometimes	never
Do you have breakfast at home?	☐	☒	☐	☐
Do you forget names?	☐	☐	☐	☒

Peter usually has breakfast at home, but he doesn't forget names.

Negative sentences
I **don't have** breakfast. He **doesn't forget** names.
→ page 137

3   I'm having a great time!

A   Sort the words in positive and negative.

+ _____   - _____

_____   _____

_____   _____

_____   _____

_____   _____

_____   _____

_____   _____

_____   _____

_____   _____

_____   _____

_____   _____

unfriendly   friendly

boring   hot and sunny

great   bad   basic

expensive   terrible

helpful   unhelpful

luxurious   excellent

interesting   cheap

cold and rainy   good

B   Pairwork. Complete the e-mail about a perfect training course.

From: anne@zoomail.com
To: teamten@jimbo.com
Re: Training

Dear all,

I'm having a _____ time! The training course is really _____

and the trainers are _____ . I'm staying in a hotel. It's

_____, and the room is very _____. At the moment I'm

sitting in an internet cafe and drinking coffee. The weather is _____.

It's always _____. The people here are very _____,

and the restaurants are _____.

I'm looking forward to seeing you next week.
Best regards,

Anne

C   Now write the negative e-mail.

4 What's important in a job?

A Look at the statistics. Are the sentences below true or false?

It's a hard life

In any case that is what the British think. A new survey compares working hours, holidays and income in five European countries, the UK, France, Germany, Spain and Italy.

Countries	UK	France	Germany	Spain	Italy
Working hours per day	8.7	7.9	8.0	8.1	7.7
Holidays per year*	28	47	41	46	44
Average hourly wage	€ 14.48	€ 13.90	€ 15.78	€ 12.57	€ 10.18
Total income	€ 54,420	€ 45,716	€ 51,675	€ 41,463	€ 36,532
Net income	€ 36,980	€ 34,345	€ 34,340	€ 29,410	€ 25,834

* including public holidays

	true	false
The British work the most but have fewer holidays than the others.	☐	☐
The Spanish have the most holidays.	☐	☐
The French have the fewest working hours per day.	☐	☐
The Germans have the highest total income.	☐	☐
The Italians work less than the French and more than the Spanish.	☐	☐

> a lot   → more   → the most
> a little → less   → the least
> a few → fewer → the fewest

B How many hours do you work?
From when to when?

I work from nine to five.

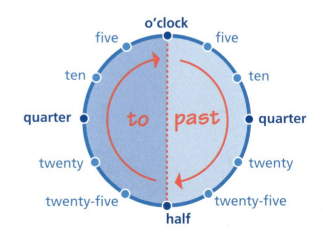

Quick Quiz

Grammar

Fill in the verbs in the correct form.

1. He _____ (be) an engineer, but at the moment he _____ (look after) his children.
2. At the moment she _____ (play) the piano.
3. At the moment they _____ (sing) in a choir.

4. _____ you _____ (need) English in your job?
5. Peter _____ (not forget) names.
6. He usually _____ (have) breakfast at home.

Vocabulary

Find the opposites. They are all in this unit.

1. always – _____
2. easy – _____
3. friendly – _____
4. cheap – _____
5. helpful – _____
6. boring – _____

Phrases

Complete the phrases with words from the unit.

1. I'm _____ a great time!
2. I'm _____ forward to seeing you.
3. _____ regards.
4. I usually work _____ nine _____ five.

Grammar: 1. is ('s), is ('s) looking after 2. is ('s) playing 3. are ('re) singing 4. Do, need 5. doesn't forget 6. has
Vocabulary: 1. never 2. hard 3. unfriendly 4. expensive 5. unhelpful 6. interesting
Phrases: 1. having 2. looking 3. Best 4. from, to

In Unit 3 haben Sie:
- gesagt, was Sie beruflich machen.
- Fragen gestellt.
- anhand einer Statistik etwas verglichen.

GRAMMATIK GRAMMATIK GRAMMATIK G

→ Present Simple und Present Continuous
→ Der unbestimmte Artikel *a / an*
→ Fragen mit *Do*
→ Stellung für Umstandsbestimmungen der Häufigkeit
→ Mengenangaben *a lot / a little / a few*

A **Was tun die abgebildeten Personen gerade? Schreiben Sie Sätze.**

1. _____
_____ .

2. _____
_____ .

3. _____
_____ .

4. _____
_____ .

5. _____
_____ .

Present Continuous oder Present Simple?
- Will man darauf hinweisen, dass eine Handlung **gerade abläuft**, wird die Present Continuous-Form verwendet, z.B. *She's **learning** Spanish at the moment.*

- Im Present Simple werden **allgemeine Aussagen** oder Handlungen ausgedrückt, die den **Normal-** bzw. **Dauerzustand** beschreibt, z.B. *He **works** in an office.*
  *I always **have** breakfast at home.*

B Schreiben Sie Sätze. Achten Sie besonders auf den unbestimmten Artikel.

1. She - engineer

_____ .

2. He - chef

_____ .

3. She - work - office

_____ .

4. They - work - farm

_____ .

5. He - work - restaurant

_____ .

6. There – internet café

_____ .

Der unbestimmte Artikel
Vor **Mitlauten** (b, c, d, usw.)   Vor **Selbstlauten** (a, e, i, o, u)
wird *a* verwendet,   benutzt man *an*,
z.B. *a good job*.   z.B. *an Italian restaurant*.

C Welche Eigenschaftswörter passen in welche Gruppe? Tragen Sie ein.
(Manche Wörter können mehrfach genannt werden.)

people   weather

_____   _____

_____   _____

_____   _____

_____   _____

_____

_____

hot
boring
famous
unfriendly
terrible
rainy
helpful
cold
friendly
sunny
interesting
unhelpful
popular

D **Schreiben Sie Aussagen über Paul und Anne.**

	always	usually	often	sometimes	never
1. read the newspaper	Paul				
2. look after the children				Anne	
3. go shopping at the weekend		Paul			
4. make breakfast					Anne
5. drink coffee				Paul	
6. go cycling			Anne		

1. _____.

2. _____.

3. _____.

4. _____.

5. _____.

6. _____.

E *Present Continuous* oder *Present Simple*? Setzen Sie die richtige Form ein.

go

not speak   do   live   be   meet   learn   like   not work

Roberta _____ from Italy, but she _____ in Scotland. She

_____ Scotland and wants to stay there, but she _____

English very well. Roberta _____ at the moment, so she _____

an intensive English course and says she _____ a lot. At the weekend

she usually _____ her friends. Sometimes they _____ hiking

in the mountains or cycling.

F **Schreiben Sie die Fragen, die zu den folgenden Aussagen passen könnten.**

1. Yes, I read a daily newspaper.

_____?

2. No, I don't have breakfast at home.

_____?

3. Yes, he enjoys his job.

_____?

4. No, she doesn't use French in her job.

_____?

5. Yes, they have an easy job.

_____?

6. No, we don't go on holiday in winter.

_____?

Mengenangaben

Zählbar	Nicht zählbar	
a few fewer restaurants the fewest	a little less money the least	the most more a lot of

---

G **Korrigieren Sie die Fehler in den Sätzen.**
Schreiben Sie das richtige Wort neben den Satz.

1. There are only a ~~little~~ shops here. _____

2. The Germans work ~~fewer~~ than the British. _____

3. The British work the most but have ~~less~~ holidays than the others. _____

4. ~~Less~~ people go on holiday in the winter than in the summer. _____

Zahlen: Punkt oder Komma?

9,99	9.99
4,5kg	4.5kg
10.000	10,000

A **Find the words**

1. In pairs, find the words in the letter chain.

usahotelitalyworkokincomehourfood

2. Create a chain of your own and give it to another pair.

B **Which country am I?**

1. Think of a country you would like to be.
2. In small groups, ask questions to find out the country.
   (You can only answer YES or NO.)

> Do you have good weather?

> Are you famous for your pasta?

> Are you Italy?

C **What's the message?**

1. Decode the following message.

```
H3
m6 n1m2's B4nd, J1m32 B4nd. I n22d 645r h21p.
m22t m2 3n th2 3nt2rn2t c1f2 1t t2n 1m.
b62

P.S.   21t th3s m2ss1g2
```

1	2	3	4	5	6
a	e	i	o	u	y

2. Now write your own coded message to a partner.
3. Then exchange messages and write a reply.

D Answer the phone

1. One person throws a ball to another person.
2. He/She then asks to speak to someone in the class.
3. The person holding the ball has to say why he/she cannot answer the phone.

I'd like to speak to Jana, please.

I'm afraid Jana ... at the moment.

4. Throw the ball until everyone has given a different excuse for another person.

writing an email

travelling to Finland

speaking to her neighbour

reading the newspaper

learning English

making coffee

working

not in

E Can you spell that, please?

1. Choose a business card.

ISUKO CORPORATION

Keizo Obuchi
Tel: (+98) 245 09 893 547

BPO International

Ms Gerrit van Wyke
Tel: (+33) 809 09 29 09

RIJ Banking Services

Mr Rhonald Blommestijn
Tel: (0441) 798 49 02

2. Close your books. Write down the name and the number your partner gives you. Then check if the spelling is correct.

D Answer the phone

1. One person throws a ball to another person.
2. He/She then asks to speak to someone in the class.
3. The person holding the ball has to say why he/she cannot answer the phone.

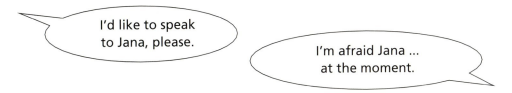

I'd like to speak to Jana, please.

I'm afraid Jana ... at the moment.

4. Throw the ball until everyone has given a different excuse for another person.

writing an email

travelling to Finland

speaking to her neighbour

reading the newspaper

learning English

making coffee

working

not in

E Can you spell that, please?

1. Choose a business card.

ISUKO CORPORATION

Keizo Obuchi
Tel: (+98) 245 09 893 547

BPO International

Ms Gerrit van Wyke

Tel: (+33) 809 09 29 09

RIJ Banking Services

Mr Rhonald Blommestijn

Tel: (0441) 798 49 02

2. Close your books. Write down the name and the number your partner gives you. Then check if the spelling is correct.

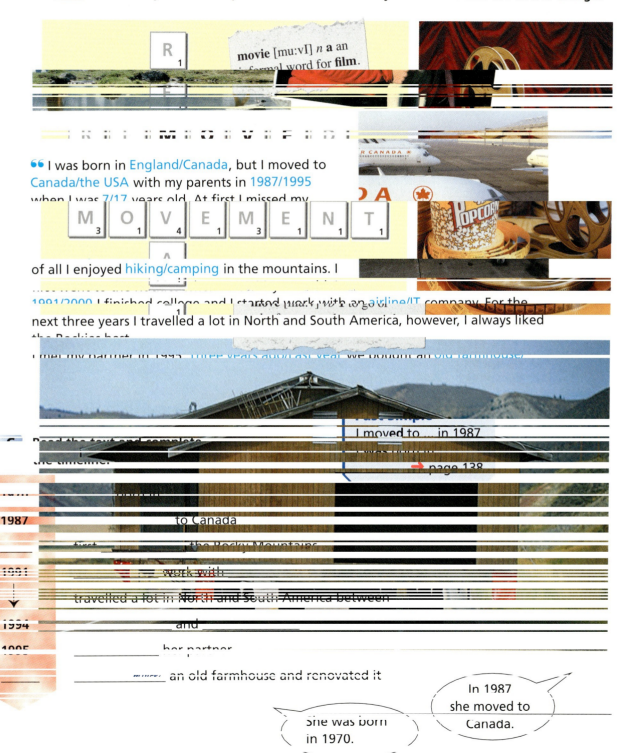

1   Moving to Canada

A   How many words and phrases with "move" do you know? Some are in the collage.

movie [muːvɪ] *n* **a** an informal word for **film**.

R
1

M O V E M E N T
3 1 4 1 3 1 1 1

❝ I was born in England/Canada, but I moved to Canada/the USA with my parents in 1987/1995 when I was 7/17 years old. At first I missed my ...

of all I enjoyed hiking/camping in the mountains. I

... 1991/2000 I finished college and I started work with an airline/IT company. For the next three years I travelled a lot in North and South America, however, I always liked the Rockies best.

I met my partner in 1993. Three years ago/Last year we bought an old farmhouse/...

I moved to ... in 1987

→ page 138

1987	to Canada
	first ... the Rocky Mountains
1991	... work with ...
↓	travelled a lot in North and South America between
1994	... and ...
1995	... her partner
	... an old farmhouse and renovated it

She was born in 1970.

In 1987 she moved to Canada.

D Pairwork. Ask and answer the questions.

	Yes	No
1. Was she born in Canada?	☐	☐
2. Was she 17 years old when she moved?	☐	☐
3. Did she meet her partner in 1991?	☐	☐
4. Did she buy an old farmhouse?	☐	☐

Past Simple: questions
Did she **move** to the USA?
Was she **born** in Canada?
➜ page 138

Yes, she was.

No, she wasn't.

Yes, she did.

No, she didn't.

E Pronunciation. Listen and practise.

1. moved ■ missed ■ learned ■ enjoyed ■ finished ■ travelled ■ liked
2. started ■ renovated

2 What's your story?

A Fill in five years that are important for you.

19___ _____
___ _____
___ _____
___ _____
___ _____

B Pairwork. Find out what your partner did.

Were you born in ...?

Did you start ...?

Past Simple: questions
Were you **born** in ...?
➜ page 138

C Now complete your timeline in A and present the most interesting fact about your partner to the class.

3 A business meeting

Tuesday
10 o'clock
meeting Charles /
performance reviews

 A **Put the dialogue in the correct order. Then listen and check.**

☐ I have a meeting with Charles, he's expecting me at 10.

☐ Good. Milk and sugar?

☐ Good morning, Jane.

☐ Yes, please, that would be great. I can look through my reviews while I'm waiting.

☐ Hello, Patricia.

☐ Milk, but no sugar, please.

☐ Oh, I'm afraid he's still in a meeting. Why don't you take a seat? Would you like a cup of coffee?

Business names

When English native speakers introduce themselves, they usually give their first name *and* their surname and people often only use first names when they talk to each other. There are, of course, always exceptions!

Employee Performance Review

Name: Amanda Clear

Started work in the ☐ purchasing department
☐ sales department

☐ works very slowly
☐ works very well in the team
☐ cannot work independently
☐ completes all tasks efficiently
☐ uses her time productively
☐ always late for meetings
☐ communicated very effectively
☐ gets on badly with the team
☐ always punctual

Adverbs
She is very **efficient**.   She works very **efficiently**.
Exception: **good** → **well**
➡ page 143

C Pairwork. Complete a negative performance review with the phrases from B.

Joe started work in the sales department.

_____

_____

_____

_____

We need to think very carefully about his future with this company.

Quick Quiz

Grammar

Fill in the correct Past Simple form.

1. I _____ (finish) college in 1991.

2. Last year we _____ (buy) an old farmhouse.

3. ● _____ she born in 1972?   ▲ Yes, she _____ .

4. ● _____ she move to the USA?   ▲ No, she _____ .

5. ● _____ you born in Canada?   ▲ No, I _____ .

Vocabulary

Find the missing adjectives/adverbs from the unit.

1. slow   –   _____

2. _____   –   well

3. careful   –   _____

4. _____   –   punctually

5. independent   –   _____

6. _____   –   badly

Phrases

Complete the phrases.

1. _____ _____ he's still in a meeting.

3. _____ _____ you take a seat?

2. _____ you _____ a cup of coffee?

4. That _____ be great.

In Unit 5 haben Sie:
- über wichtige Stationen in Ihrem Leben gesprochen.
- jemanden zu seiner/ihrer Vergangenheit befragen.
- Geschäftsbesuch empfangen.
- eine kurze Beurteilung geschrieben.

GRAMMATIK GRAMMATIK GRAMMATIK GRAM

→ Past Simple (regelmäßige und unregelmäßige Zeitwörter)
→ Kurzantworten in der Vergangenheit
→ Fragen mit *Did*, *Was* und *Were*
→ Adverbien

A **Ergänzen Sie die Kurzantworten passend zu den folgenden Fragen.**

1. ● Did you start work after you finished school?

   ▲ Yes, _____.

2. ● Did you enjoy school?

   ▲ No, _____. I wasn't good at school!

3. ● Did you get a good job after you finished school?

   ▲ Yes, _____. My first job was working in an office.

4. ● Were you happy when you moved to Chicago?

   ▲ Yes, _____. It was very exciting.

5. ● Did you miss your home at first?

   ▲ No, _____. Not really.

6. ● Did you start work after you moved to Chicago?

   ▲ No, _____. But a few months later I got a job with a travel

   agency. It was great!

7. ● Were you happy living and working in the USA?

   ▲ Oh, yes, _____. It's a fantastic place!

B Setzen Sie die Verben in der richtigen Form ein.

start · meet · be · renovate · be · start

move · finish · be · work · go · buy · be

Meeting in the USA

David _____ born in Hong Kong in 1971. He _____ school in Hong Kong in 1976. He _____ school when he _____ 18, and a little later he moved to the USA, first to New York, then to San Francisco.

Sarah _____ born in the USA and _____ to school there. Her father is American, her mother _____ born in Vietnam in 1943. In 1965 her mother's family _____ to the USA.

Last year David and Sarah _____ in San Francisco. They both _____ at the same restaurant. Three months ago they _____ a house in San Francisco and _____ it together. Sarah, her mother, and John _____ their own restaurant two weeks ago.

Past Simple
- Bei den meisten Zeitwörtern wird die Vergangenheit gebildet, indem an die Grundform des Zeitworts **-ed** angehängt wird *(work – worked)*. Endet ein Zeitwort auf **-e**, wird nur **-d** angehängt *(move – moved)*.
- Dagegen haben unregelmäßige Zeitwörter eine eigene Vergangenheitsform: z.B. *be – was/were, go – went*.

C **Bilden Sie anhand der Stichworte Fragen.**

1. go to school in England

   Did you go _____?

2. like school

   _____?

3. enjoy travelling when you were young

   _____?

4. happy in England

   _____?

5. work for a travel company in Chicago

   _____?

6. your job interesting

   _____?

7. meet your partner in Chicago

   _____?

8. have your own flat

   _____?

D **Wie reagieren Sie in den folgenden Situationen?**
Kreuzen Sie die jeweils <u>höflichste</u> Anwort an.

🇬🇧 flat
🇺🇸 apartment

1. Good morning, Susan.

   ☐ Good morning.   ☐ It's afternoon!

2. How are you?

   ☐ OK.   ☐ Fine, thanks.

3. Why don't you take a seat?

☐ I don't want a seat.   ☐ Thanks.

4. I'm afraid Mr Smith is in a meeting. Would you like a cup of coffee?

☐ Yes.   ☐ Yes, please.

5. Milk and sugar?

☐ No.   ☐ No, thanks.

6. By the way, this is Ms Goodall.

☐ Hi.   ☐ Nice to meet you, Ms Goodall.

Adjektive – Adverbien

- Adjektive (Eigenschaftswörter) geben genauere Informationen über Personen oder Sachen, z.B. *an **efficient** employee*
  *a **productive** meeting*

- Adverbien (Umstandswörter) dagegen geben genauere Informationen über das Zeitwort. Ein Adverb wird gebildet, indem *-ly* an das Adjektiv angehängt wird: *She works **efficiently**.*

E **Adverb oder Adjektiv? Markieren Sie die richtige Form.**

1. Anna is **great / greatly**. She always works so **efficient / efficiently**.

2. John gets on very **bad / badly** with the team. It's **terrible / terribly**.

3. Sarah always finishes her tasks **punctual / punctually** and she's very
   productive / productively, too.

4. Paul is never **punctual / punctually**. Yesterday he arrived **late / lately**
   for a meeting with the boss. And he's a very **slow / slowly** worker, too.

5. Susan never needs help with her work. She is very **independent / independently**.

6. She's quite **good / well** at volleyball, but she doesn't play tennis very **good / well**.

Late als Adverb
Manche Adjektive haben als Adverb die gleiche Form, z.B. *He always arrives **late**.* Würde man hier die Endung *-ly* anhängen, so würde sich dadurch die Bedeutung verändern: *lately* – kürzlich, in letzter Zeit.

Then and now

1 What did we do before ...?

A Brainstorm things you have that your grandparents did not have.

Then ...

and now

a car

a mobile phone

a dishwasher

a computer

B **Complete the sentences.**

wrote letters

read books

went to the theatre

had a quiet/busy life

grew vegetables

made our own bread

did everything by hand

got around by bike

1. Before e-mail we _*wrote letters.*_____

2. Before machines we _____

3. Before supermarkets we _____

4. Before mobile phones we _____

5. Before bakeries we _____

6. Before television we _____

7. Before cars we _____

C **What did your grandparents do / not do when they were young?**

They wrote letters.

They didn't watch television.

They ...

The Amish

The Amish are a very religious community who live mainly in Pennsylvania, USA. The first Amish people came to America from Germany nearly 300 years ago and the Amish today still speak German dialect and have the same old-fashioned way of life. Many of them have no modern machines, cars, phones and even electricity. Amish children walk to school, there is no school bus to take them there. For the Amish their family and their religion are the most important things in life.

2 First jobs

A Listen to the interview and number the questions in the order you hear them.

☐ Did you have your own office?

☐ How long did you work there?

☐ How did you contact people before e-mail?

☐ When did you get your first computer and fax machine?

☐ How did you copy documents before photocopiers?

☐ What did you do when you left school?

☐ Did you like your job?

☐ What did you do?

☐ Do you still work in an office today?

> **Past Simple: Questions**
> **How long did** you **work** there?
> **What did** you **do?**
> **How/When did** you ...?
> → page 138

B Listen again. Are the statements true or false?

	true	false
1. She found a job at an IT company.	☐	☐
2. She started work in 1976.	☐	☐
3. It wasn't very interesting.	☐	☐
4. Nowadays she sends more e-mails than faxes.	☐	☐
5. She got her first computer in 1968.	☐	☐
6. Photocopiers were very cheap in those days.	☐	☐

C Pairwork. Find out about your partner.

What did you do when you left school?

What did you do?

Did you like it?

3 Mobile phones

A Read what the people think about mobile phones. Mark the statements
(+ = positive, – = negative)

Nowadays you hear phones ringing in the cinema, in restaurants, on the bus. I don't want to hear everyone's phone conversations. Yesterday I was having lunch with a friend in a really nice restaurant when her phone suddenly rang. Unbelievable! I think people should turn off their phones in public places, especially when they are with other people. ☐

I bought a mobile for my daughter when she was 14 years old. She can always contact me and tell me where she is – that's very important. I like to know she's safe. My daughter can use her mobile from a safe place and phone a taxi. I don't want her walking on dark streets looking for a telephone box. ☐

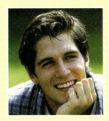

My mobile is essential for my work. I need a mobile to call my clients to tell them when I am coming. Sometimes a visit is cancelled last minute or there is an emergency, like last night. A client called while I was driving home and I had to make an unplanned visit. My mobile saves me a lot of time. ☐

I think mobiles are too expensive. They are very easy to use, and then the phone bill just gets bigger and bigger. I have a phone at home and in the office and people can contact me in those two places, but when I'm in the theatre or visiting friends I want to enjoy my time. I don't want to talk on the phone all the time. ☐

> **Past Continuous**
> I **was having** lunch with a friend **when** her phone suddenly **rang**.
> A client **called while** I **was driving** home.
>
> ➔ page 138

B Tick what the people use their mobile phone for.

☐	call a taxi	☐	call clients
☐	make appointments	☐	take a photo
☐	surf the internet	☐	phone a friend
☐	phone home	☐	send text messages

C What do you think about mobile phones.

I think mobile phones are …

My mobile is …

I bought a mobile …

I agree. I think …

I don't agree.

'It's a shelter for making calls from when it rains.'

4 Pronunciation

  A Listen and practise.

1. vegetables – television – very – conversation – expensive – visiting
2. dishwasher – work – what – when – with - walking – want

Quick Quiz

Then and now

Grammar

Complete the questions.

1. _____ long _____ you live there?
2. _____ did you do?
3. _____ did you start your first job?
4. _____ did you contact people?

Fill in the Past Continuous form.

5. I_____ _____ lunch with a friend, when her mobile phone suddenly _____ .

Vocabulary

Find the Past Simple form.

1. write _____
2. buy _____
3. do _____
4. go _____
5. grow _____
6. read _____

Phrases

Complete the phrases with verbs from the unit.

1. _____ everything by hand
2. _____ a quiet life
3. _____ your own bread
4. _____ around by bike

Phrases: 1. do 2. have 3. make 4. get
Vocabulary: 1. wrote 2. bought 3. did 4. went 5. grew 6. read
Grammar: 1. How, did 2. What 3. When 4. How 5. was having, rang

In Unit 6 haben Sie:
- über Früher gesprochen.
- über Ihren ersten Job gesprochen.
- Fragen zum ersten Job gestellt.
- Ihre Meinung zu Mobiltelefonen gesagt und die Vor- und Nachteile diskutiert.

GRAMMATIK GRAMMATIK GRAM

➜ Past Simple (unregelmäßige Zeitwörter)
➜ Fragen im Past Simple
➜ Past Continuous

A Setzen Sie die Zeitwörter in der Vergangenheitsform ein.

That's life

When my father _____ (be) young, he and his family _____ (live) on a farm. He _____ (go) to school when he was five, but in the afternoon when he _____ (come) home he _____ (work) on the farm. His family _____ (grow) their own vegetables and _____ (have) animals. It _____ (be) a hard life because his family _____ (not have) a lot of money. When he _____ (finish) school my father was 15. When he was 20 he _____ (leave) England and _____ (go) to the USA. He _____ (not find) work at first. However, when my father _____ (meet) my mother, he _____ (start) work with her father – on his farm!

B Bilden Sie zu jeder Antwort mit Hilfe der Wörter in den Kreisen eine passende Frage. Nehmen Sie aus jedem Kreis ein Wort / eine Wendung.

1. ● _____?

   ▲ I lived there for two years.

2. ● _____?

   ▲ First I travelled, then I worked.

3. ● _____?

   ▲ I asked people, looked at the internet, read the newspaper.

4. ● _____?

   ▲ In a small flat.

5. ● _____?

   ▲ I came back two months ago.

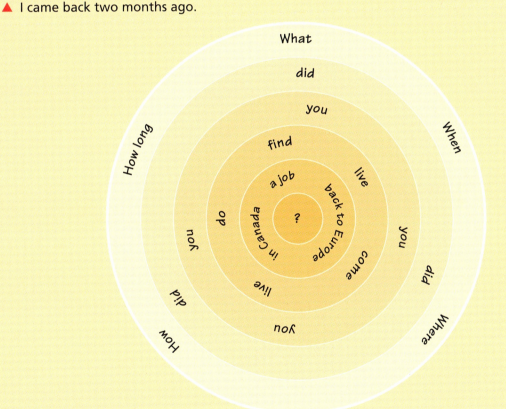

Past Simple
Die Past Simple-Form drückt eine abgeschlossene Handlung in der Vergangenheit aus.
Daher kommt diese Zeitform häufig in Verbindung mit Zeitangaben wie *(300 years)* **ago**, **in** *(1976)*, **last** *(year)*, **before** *(e-mails)* usw. vor.

C Vervollständigen Sie die Fragen.

1. ● _____ after school?

   ▲ I worked in an office.

2. ● _____ start work there?

   ▲ In 1996.

3. ● _____ there?

   ▲ I worked there for about two years.

4. ● _____?

   ▲ What I did? I wrote letters and answered the phone.

5. ● _____ to England?

   ▲ Last year - I moved back to England last year.

6. ● _____ are you?

   ▲ I'm 27 years old.

D *Past Simple* oder *Past Continuous*? Setzen Sie das Zeitwort in der richtigen Zeitform ein.

1. I _____ lunch when they _____ to cancel the meeting. (have, call)

2. He _____ the newspaper when she _____ home from work. (read, come)

3. I _____ him while I _____ home from work. (meet, walk)

4. He _____ an e-mail when the telephone _____. (write, ring)

5. Yesterday my mobile _____ to ring while I _____ to some customers. (start, talk)

6. He _____ breakfast when his mother _____. (have, arrive)

7. I _____ for a taxi when someone _____ me where the cinema was. (wait, ask)

Past Continuous
Spricht man von zwei gleichzeitigen Handlungen in der Vergangenheit, so wird das Past Continuous für die längere und das Past Simple für die kürzere Handlung benutzt.

her phone suddenly rang
↓
I was having lunch with a friend

E Was kann man in der Freizeit alles tun? Tragen Sie das durcheinander geratene Wort in das Gitter ein und finden Sie das Lösungswort.

1. I meet my erinsdf.
2. I go to the treteah.
3. I play tnisen.
4. I tvealr a lot.
5. I do storp.
6. I go on hlaoyid.
7. I go cgainmp.
8. I often go to the camine.

F Regelmäßig oder unregelmäßig? Tragen Sie die Zeitwörter in die richtige Spalte ein.

do   enjoy   move   learn   go   start   buy   meet   finish

be   travel   write   have   walk   talk   make   get

read   find   call

Regular

_____   _____   _____   _____

_____   _____   _____   _____

_____

Irregular

_____   _____   _____   _____

_____   _____   _____   _____

_____   _____   _____

Unit 7
Holidays

cruise

1 **Before you go**

city break

beach holiday

camping

A **What kind of holiday(s) do you like?**

I like beach holidays.

So do I.

Neither do I.

I don't like beach holidays.

I prefer cruises.

B **What do you have to do before your holiday? Write as many words as possible next to the verbs.**

book	*hotel, tickets,* _____	car rental
(tele)phone	_____	
pack	_____	hotel
buy	_____	
organize	_____	suitcase
check	_____	
collect	_____	visas
make	_____	
cancel	_____	sun cream

newspaper   checklist   dentist's appointment   travel agent   tickets

C Read the checklist and listen.
Tick what they have done.

234 1122 -
travel agent

Things to do
- book the hotel
- phone the travel agent
- organize the car rental
- collect the tickets
- check the tickets
- pack
- buy a suitcase
- cancel the newspaper

D Report. What have they done? What haven't they done?

They haven't ... They've ...	phoned
	packed
	bought
	collected
	cancelled
	checked
	organized

Present Perfect
They**'ve** (have) **booked** the hotel.
They **haven't** (have not) **booked** the hotel.
→ page 138

2   A dentist's appointment

OAKLEY DENTAL SURGERY

Dr William Kent & Associates

5 Oakley Lane
Oakley
MN25 6PT

Tel. 763 5484

| Surgery Hours: | Mon. – Fri. | 8.30 am – 5.30 pm |
| Evening Appointments: | Mon. & Tues. | 6.30 pm – 8.30 pm |

A   Read the beginning of the dialogue and number the other sentences in the correct order.

■ Good afternoon, Oakley Dental Surgery.

▲ Hello. I'd like to make an appointment with Dr Kent, please.

■ Certainly. Have you been here before?

▲ Yes. My name's Martha Burns.

☐ Well, we could fit you in this evening.

☐ Bye.

☐ Yes, that's OK. Thanks very much.

☐ Yes, that's fine. What time?

☐ Oh yes, Mrs Burns. Let me check. What about Friday, 13th at two thirty?

☐ You're welcome. Goodbye.

☐ Oh, I'm afraid I can't make Friday, 13th. I'm going on holiday on the 12th and would like a check-up before I go.

☐ Would five thirty be convenient?

| 14:30 | **two thirty** = half past two |
| **Friday 13th** | Friday **the** thirteenth |

B   Listen and check.

C Pronunciation. Listen and practise.

1. Friday, 13th at two thirty
2. Monday, 5th at ten fifteen
3. Thursday 31st at nine o'clock
4. Wednesday, 12th at six

D Role play. Make an appointment.

> ℹ️
> 1st   -   first
> 2nd   -   second
> 3rd   -   third
> 4th   -   fourth
> 5th   -   fifth

3 What have you done today?

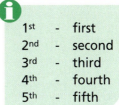

Have you smiled today?

A Note three things you have done today.

1. _____
2. _____
3. _____

I've been to the dentist.

B Pairwork. Find something in common.

> ℹ️
> She's gone to the dentist. →
> She's been to the dentist. ⇄

Have you been to the dentist today?

Yes, I have.

No, I haven't.

C Report.

We've both been to the dentist today.

> **Present Perfect**
> She **hasn't made** an appointment yet.
> ➡️ page 138

5 Road Trips

A Number the paragraphs in the correct order.

Route 66, Arizona, USA

❑ Dan and Sandy Applegate are two avid road trippers and have just bought a new motorhome. "This is our 41st road trip and we're having a great time," says Sandy. They said they loved driving and their favourite road trip routes were along Route 66, from Chicago to Los Angeles, and from coast to coast.

❑ For people who are thinking about their first road trip, there are lots of interesting internet sites all about road tripping which give advice, travel tips and general information.

❑ A very popular kind of vacation in the USA is the road trip. Every summer thousands of Americans go on a road trip in their cars or motorhomes. The idea is usually to see as much of America as possible in the time available - a weekend, one week or a few months. Road trippers sometimes drive hundreds of miles in a day. They drive through and across the different States and stop at as many towns, cities and attractions along the way as they can.

ℹ 🇬🇧 holiday
🇺🇸 vacation

Reported speech
Dan and Sandy Applegate: "We love driving."
They **said** they **loved** driving.
➡ page 144

B Report what they said.

1. "This is our 41st road trip."

   She said _____

2. "We're having a great time.

   She said _____

3. "Our favourite road trip routes are along Route 66."

   They said _____

Quick Quiz

Grammar

Fill in the correct Present Perfect form.

1. They _____ (book) the hotel.

2. They _____ (not buy) a suitcase.

3. _____ you _____ (be) to the dentist?

4. Yes, I _____.

5. No, I _____.

Complete the sentence in Reported Speech.

6. They said they _____ _____ a great time.

Vocabulary

Fill in the missing words.

1. _____ break

2. _____ agent

3. _____ rental

4. _____ cream

5. _____ appointment

6. _____ trip

Phrases

Complete the phrases with words from the unit.

1. ■ I like beach holidays.

   ▲ _____ do I.

2. ■ I don't like city breaks.

   ▲ _____ do I.

3. Would half past two be _____?

4. We could _____ you _____ this evening.

5. I'm _____ I can't _____ Thursday 12th.

6. _____ _____ _____ make an appointment.

In Unit 7 haben Sie:
- gesagt, welche Art von Urlaub Sie bevorzugen und was Sie nicht so gerne tun.
- jemandem zugestimmt.
- gesagt, was Sie schon erledigt bzw. gemacht haben.
- telefonisch einen Termin vereinbart.

GRAMMATIK GRAMMATIK GRAMMATIK G

➜ Present Perfect (Kurzantworten, Verneinung, Fragen)
➜ Uhrzeiten
➜ Indirekte Rede

A Suchen Sie die Zeitwörter im Partizip Perfekt und tragen Sie sie in die letzte Spalte ein.

comegrowngonedonegothadleftbeen

	Grundform	Vergangenheitsform	Partizip Perfekt
1.	go	went	_____
2.	do	did	_____
3.	leave	left	_____
4.	get	got	_____
5.	grow	grew	_____
6.	be	was / were	_____
7.	have	had	_____
8.	come	came	_____

Present Perfect (1)

- Das Present Perfect wird mit dem Verb *have* und dem Partizip Perfekt gebildet, z.B. *She **has booked** (the hotel)*.

- Bei regelmäßigen Verben sind die Past Simple-Form und das Partizip Perfekt gleich, z.B. *book – book**ed** – book**ed***.

- Das Zeitwort *have* wird in der gesprochenen Sprache in der Regel in der Kurzform gesprochen: *I've, you've* etc.

- Fragen im Present Perfect werden gebildet, indem der Aussagesatz einfach umgedreht wird: *She has booked the hotel. – Has she booked the hotel?*

B Vergleichen Sie die Checklisten und vervollständigen Sie die Sätze.

Tom

> ✓ collect the tickets
> ✓ phone my parents
> buy food for the journey
> ✓ cancel the newspaper
> pack my suitcase

Anita

> ✓ phone my parents
> buy food for the journey
> ✓ cancel the newspaper
> ✓ pack my suitcase
> organize the taxi to the station

1. Tom has _____ .

2. They've both _____ .

3. They haven't _____ .

4. They've both _____ .

5. Anita _____ .

6. Tom _____ .

7. Anita _____ .

C Schreiben Sie die Uhrzeiten in Worten auf. Geben Sie gegebenenfalls beide Formen an.

1. 13:30 `h` `a` `l` `f` `p` `a` `s` `t` `o` `n` `e`
   □□□ □□□□□□

2. 8:00 □□□□□ `o'`□□□□□

3. 12:15 □□□□□□□ □□□□□ □□□□□□
   □□□□□□□ □□□□□ □□□□

4. 3:45 □□□□□ □□ □□□□
   □□□□□□ □□□□□□-□□□□

5. 3:00 □□□□□ `'`□□□□□□

6. 21:45 □□□□□□ □□ □□□
   □□□□ □□□□□□-□□□□

7. 11:30 □□□□ □□□□ □□□□□□
   □□□□□□ □□□□□

Practice Section

D Ergänzen Sie die Fragen mit dem passenden Zeitwort
in der richtigen Form.

Would you please:
— read my e-mail
— cancel the meeting with Dr O'Neill
— write the letters
— find the documents for the meeting on Friday
— make an appointment with Mr Smith
— phone the travel agency

1. Have you _____ my e-mail?

2. Have you _____ the meeting with Dr O'Neill?

3. Have you _____ the letters?

4. Have you _____ the documents for the meeting on Friday?

5. Have you _____ an appointment with Mr Smith?

6. Have you _____ the travel agency?

> **Present Perfect (2)**
> Das Present Perfect wird häufig benutzt, um über eine Handlung in der
> Vergangenheit zu sprechen, wenn der genaue Zeitpunkt nicht wichtig ist.
> Entscheidend ist, ob man etwas **schon** oder **schon einmal** gemacht hat bzw.,
> bei verneinten Sätzen, etwas **noch nicht** gemacht hat.

E Setzen Sie die fehlenden Wörter in den Dialog ein.

great	in	Would	make	afraid	Let	What	fit

● I'd like to _____ an appointment, please.

▲ Yes, certainly. _____ me check. What about Thursday 4th?

● Oh, I'm _____ I can't make Thursday.

▲ Well, we could _____ you _____ tomorrow morning.

● Yes, that's fine. _____ time?

▲ _____ nine thirty be convenient?

● Yes, that's _____.

▲ What's the name, please?

F Bringen Sie die folgenden Aussagen über eine Reise nach England in die indirekte Rede.

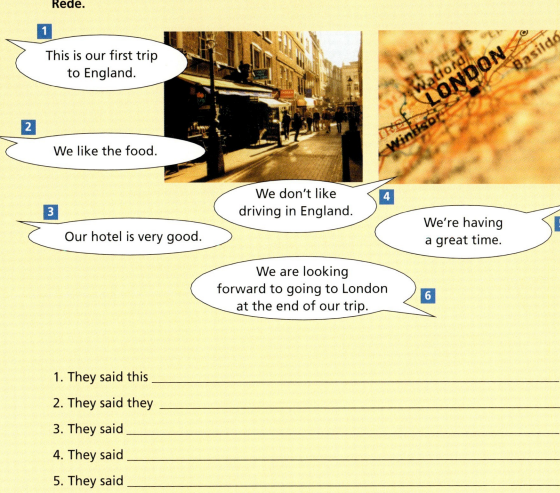

1 This is our first trip to England.

2 We like the food.

4 We don't like driving in England.

3 Our hotel is very good.

5 We're having a great time.

6 We are looking forward to going to London at the end of our trip.

1. They said this _____ .

2. They said they _____ .

3. They said _____ .

4. They said _____ .

5. They said _____ .

6. They said _____

_____ .

Reported Speech (indirekte Rede)

Um etwas zu berichten, was in der Vergangenheit gesagt wurde, beginnt man den Satz im Past Simple (z.B. *She said* ...). Stand das Zeitwort des wiedergegebenen Satzes in der Present Simple-Form, wird es ebenfalls ins Past Simple gesetzt:

"We love driving."
They **said** they lov**ed** driving.

Revision

A **Pack the suitcase**

1. Think of one thing you take on holiday.
2. The first person says what he/she has packed.
3. Everyone adds something to the suitcase.

> I've packed the sun cream.

> She's packed the sun cream, I've packed the passports.

> She's packed the sun cream, he's packed the passports, and I've packed …

B **Mime an activity**

1. Mime an activity from the first half of the book.
2. The others guess what the activity is.

> You're reading a book.

> No, you're reading the newspaper.

C **Where were you?**

1. Form small groups. The first person gives the beginning of a question.
2. The second person adds the next word, the third person another word etc.
3. When the question is complete, the next person tries to answer the question.

How   Did   Was   Were   What   When

D — Tell a story

1. In small groups write a story. All the things in the pictures must be in the story.

2. Now tell your story.

E — Words

1. **Work in small groups. Choose three words.**
2. **On a piece of paper draw your first word, describe your second word in English, translate your third word into your language.**

bread / Tuesday / holiday

1. _____

2. The second working day of the week: _____

    _____

3. Urlaub/Ferien: _____

3. **Now exchange pieces of paper and guess the other group's words.**

Unit 9

A trip down under

1 Planning a trip

Darwin

Kakadu
National Park

Great Barrier Reef

Cairns

Great Barrier Reef

Broome

The Bungle
Bungles

Wet Tropics of
Queensland

Mackay

Alice Springs

Yulara

Ayers Rock

Rockhan

Shark
Bay

Coober
Pedy

BRISB

Pinnacles Desert

Nullarbor Plain

Darling

The Blue
Mountain

PERTH

ADELAIDE

Murray

SYDNEY

CANBERRA

Kangaroo
Island

MELBOURNE

Uluru or Ayers Rock?

Uluru is the traditional Aboriginal
name for Ayers Rock and the one
the local Anangu Aboriginal people
prefer everyone to use.

72

A Read the e-mail and draw the route on the map.

To: **Sheila**
From: **Bruce**   Date:
Re: **Travel plans**

Hi Sheila,
Here's the plan for our trip round Australia:

You're arriving in Brisbane on Monday and we're staying in a hotel on Monday night.

Early on Tuesday we're collecting the motorhome and we're driving about 1000km up the coast to Mackay. From Wednesday to Saturday we're staying in Mackay and on the Friday we're taking a boat trip to the Barrier Reef.

From Sunday to the following Thursday we're travelling across the Outback to Yulara near Uluru (Ayers Rock). We're camping for four nights in Yulara and we're visiting Uluru for the day on the Friday.

At the beginning of our last week we're leaving the motorhome in Alice Springs and flying to Perth on Tuesday morning. On the Tuesday afternoon we're taking the Indian Pacific Railway to Sydney. I'm booking a great restaurant for the Friday night when we arrive. On Saturday we're sightseeing in Sydney and in the evening we're going to the opera.

Looking forward to seeing you.

Bruce

P.S. If you have any questions, you can call me at home.

Future: Present Continuous
You**'re arriving** in Brisbane on Monday.
In the evening we**'re going** to the opera.
→ page 140

B Tick the means of transport they are using on their trip.

☐ train   ☐ car   ☐ bus   ☐ motorhome
☐ plane   ☐ ferry   ☐ boat   ☐ bicycle

C Group work. You have three weeks in Australia. Create your own trip.

Let's take the Indian Pacific from Perth to Sydney.

I'd like to visit Coober Pedy.

Why don't we go hiking in the Blue Mountains?

	week 1	week 2	week 3
Monday			
Tuesday			
Wednesday			
Thursday			
Friday			
Saturday			
Sunday			

D Present your trip to the class.

In week 1 we're travelling to Perth.

We're visiting Uluru in week 2.

2 Booking a motorhome

A Match the words to the areas of the motorhome.

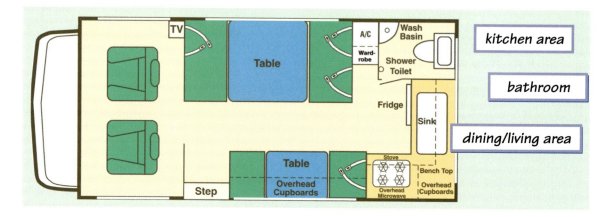

kitchen area

bathroom

dining/living area

B Read the adverts and look at the form. Which motorhome would you recommend?

Elite motorhome
From $55/day

Ideal for two people. This comfortable motorhome comes with a large dining area which converts into a large double bed. Extras include camping chairs.

Country Club

From $120/day

This motorhome is ideal for up to four adults. This spacious motorhome comes with a large living area and plenty of storage space. It includes two double beds and two single beds. The Country Club has a microwave, hot and cold water, and a shower and toilet. Extras include a camping table and chairs.

The Regent

From $170/day

This motorhome has everything the Elite and Country Club motorhomes have and more. It can accommodate up to four adults and two children with two double beds and two single beds. Extras include two mountain bikes, a colour TV and video.

All motorhomes have air conditioning. Standard equipment includes a gas stove, a fridge with freezer, crockery and cutlery, cooking utensils and cold water.

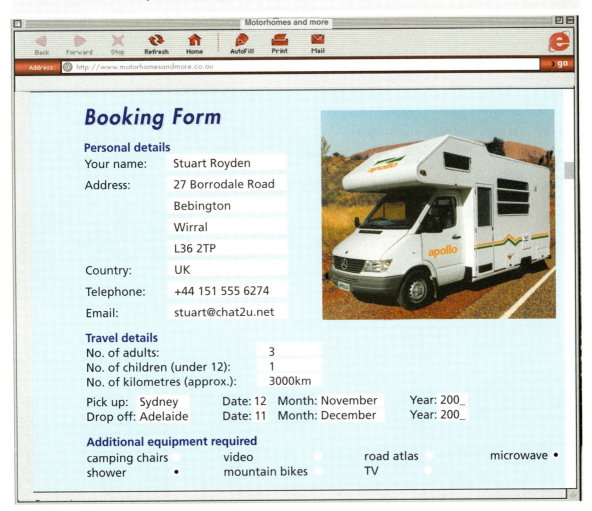

Motorhomes and more

Back   Forward   Stop   Refresh   Home   AutoFill   Print   Mail

Address: @ http://www.motorhomesandmore.co.au   › go

Booking Form

Personal details

Your name: Stuart Royden

Address: 27 Borrodale Road

Bebington

Wirral

L36 2TP

Country: UK

Telephone: +44 151 555 6274

Email: stuart@chat2u.net

Travel details

No. of adults: 3
No. of children (under 12):   1
No. of kilometres (approx.):   3000km

Pick up: Sydney   Date: 12   Month: November   Year: 200_
Drop off: Adelaide   Date: 11   Month: December   Year: 200_

Additional equipment required

| camping chairs | | video | | road atlas | | microwave | • |
| shower | • | mountain bikes | | TV | | | |

75

Complete the dialogue with the questions. Then listen and check.

> how much
> is that

> when do you
> want to travel

> how many
> kilometres are you
> travelling

> how can
> I help you

> which
> motorhome
> would you like

> how many people
> are travelling

▲ Good morning, Motorhomes and More, _____?

■ Hello, I'd like to make a booking, please.

▲ Certainly, _____?

■ I'd like to book the Regent for two weeks.

▲ OK, _____?

■ From 20th August until 3rd September.

▲ OK, and _____?

■ Two adults and three children.

▲ And approximately _____?

■ About 3000.

▲ So that's two weeks, 3000 kilometres, from 20th August until 3rd September.

■ Yes, that's right. And _____?

▲ That's AUS$1900 all inclusive.

> **Quantifiers**
> **How many** people are travelling?
> **How much** (money) is it?
> → page 144

D **Role play. Book a motorhome.**

3   Do's and don'ts of driving in Australia

A   **Match and compare with a partner.**

Make sure	1. _____ a seat belt.
Watch out	2. _____ for kangaroos.
Travel	3. _____ on the left.
Wear	4. _____ and drive.
Drive	5. _____ that your driving licence is valid.
Check	6. _____ you have enough petrol.
Don't drink	7. _____ with plenty of water.

B   **Pronounciation. Listen and practise.**

1. motorhome
2. approximately
3. microwave
4. kilometres
5. kangaroo
6. Australia

> **Imperative**
> **Wear** a seat belt.
> **Don't drink** and **drive**.
> → page 145

Grammar

Complete the sentences.

1. We _____ (stay) in a hotel on Monday night.

2. How many kilometres _____ you _____ (travel)?

3. How _____ people are travelling?

4. How _____ is that?

5. _____ out for kangaroos.

6. _____ drink and drive.

Vocabulary

Complete the words.

1. b ☐ d
2. s h ☐ w ☐ r
3. k ☐ t c h ☐ n

4. f r ☐ d g ☐
5. m ☐ c r ☐ w ☐ v ☐
6. t ☐ ☐ l ☐ t

Phrases

Complete the phrases.

1. looking _____ to seeing you

2. _____ the beginning

3. early _____ Tuesday

4. _____ Wednesday _____ Saturday

5. _____ the evening

GRAMMATIK GRAMMATIK GRA

→ *Present Continuous* als Zukunftsform
→ (How) much / many
→ Befehlsform

A **Setzen Sie die Zeitwörter in der Verlaufsform ein.**

1. Next week we _____ to Verona to the opera, and the next day we _____. (go, sightsee)

2. Sorry, I can't come to your party on Saturday because I _____ my parents. (visit)

3. What _____ you _____ on Thursday evening? We _____ a little party here. Can you come? (do, have)

4. On Saturday I _____ tennis in the afternoon, but I can come and see you in the evening. (play)

5. We _____ to London in the morning, and _____ shopping. But we can meet in the evening. (drive, go)

6. They've cancelled my flight, so I _____ the train instead. (take)

B Vervollständigen Sie den Text mit den Angaben aus dem Kalenderauszug.

Monday	*play golf with Barbara*
Tuesday	*visit George in hospital*
Wednesday	*collect the tickets from the travel agency*
Thursday	*go to the opera with Daniel*
Friday	*pack my suitcase*
Saturday	*go to Berlin*
Sunday	*Berlin*

> Let's go to the pub after work some time next week.

"I'm sorry, but I'm really busy next week.

On Monday I'm _____.

On Tuesday _____.

On Wednesday _____.

On Thursday _____.

On Friday _____.

At the weekend _____.

Why don't we make it the week after? Say ... Tuesday or Wednesday evening? ..."

Present Continuous als Zukunftsform

- Das Present Continuous wird als Zukunftsform benutzt, wenn man über Vereinbarungen und Pläne für die nähere Zukunft spricht:
  We're staying at a hotel on Monday night.

- Die Present Continuous-Form kennen Sie schon als Verlaufsform der Gegenwart (siehe Unit 3), z.B. *She's learning Spanish at the moment.*

C *Much* oder *many*? Setzen Sie die richtige Form in die Fragen ein.

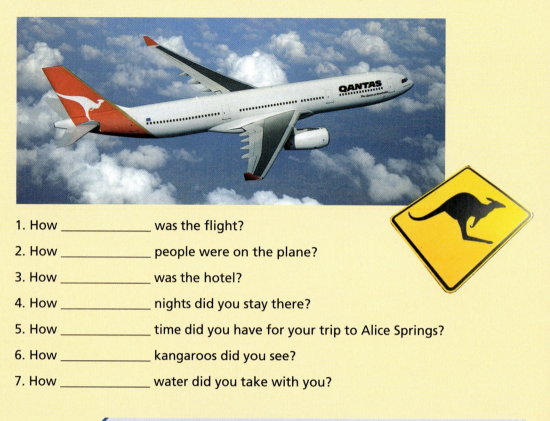

1. How _____ was the flight?

2. How _____ people were on the plane?

3. How _____ was the hotel?

4. How _____ nights did you stay there?

5. How _____ time did you have for your trip to Alice Springs?

6. How _____ kangaroos did you see?

7. How _____ water did you take with you?

> **Much / many**
> **Many** wird mit Wörtern verwendet, die „zählbar" sind, d.h. vor die man eine Zahl stellen kann, z.B. *kilometres, people*.
> **Much** verwendet man mit „nicht zählbaren" Begriffen, z.B. *money*.

D Vervollständigen Sie die gut gemeinten „Ratschläge" von Bruce an Sheila.

1. _____ a flight to Brisbane.

2. _____ your ticket before you go.

3. _____ your passport.

4. _____ sure your driving licence is valid.

5. _____ for the plane.

6. _____ me from the airport.

> Don't forget

> Book   Call

> Make   Check

> Don't be late

> **Befehlsform**
> In Befehlssätzen wird die Grundform des Zeitwortes benutzt. Verneinte Aufforderungen werden mit *don't* (*do not*) und der Grundform des Zeitwortes gebildet.

E Jeweils eines der fünf Wörter passt nicht in die Reihe. Markieren Sie es.

1. table	microwave	chair	cupboard	wardrobe
2. wine	water	milk	tea	cheese
3. seat belt	car	flight	drive	driving licence
4. stove	microwave	sink	fridge	colour TV
5. bicycle	car	motorhome	bus	taxi
6. sightseeing	restaurant	boat trip	office	opera

Motorhome
Wenn Sie in Australien ein Wohnmobil mieten wollen, finden
Sie dies in der Regel unter dem Begriff *motorhome*.
Es gibt aber auch andere Bezeichnungen, z.B. *camper, camper
van, motor caravan* oder *RV* (kurz für *recreational vehicle*).

F Vervollständigen Sie den Dialog.

How much   So that's   when   How many

what's   I'd like   can

▲ Royal Hotel, good morning, _____ I help you?

■ Good morning. _____ to book a room, please.

▲ Yes, certainly. Double or single?

■ A double room, please.

▲ And _____ is it for?

■ 15th of June.

▲ _____ nights, please?

■ Five nights. _____is it?

▲ $40 per night, so $200 in total.

■ OK. That's fine.

▲ _____ one double room for five nights, arriving on June 15th.

■ That's right.

▲ And _____ the name, please?

Eating out

1 **How about Indian?**

Molly Malone's
Irish Restaurant & Bar

Traditional Food
Music &
Atmosphere
Live Music

Weekends Open 7 days till late
6 King Street, Parnell, Auckland

MOCCA
café – restaurant – bar
breakfast – lunch – dinner
open 7am till late – 7 days
waterfall plaza
canal basin – ph 555 1093

Cherry Blossom Restaurant
– Taste of Japan –

OPEN 365 DAYS
FULLY LICENSED

LEMON GRASS
24 New South Rd
Superb Thai Cuisine.
Licensed Restaurant.

Lunch: Monday to Saturday.
Dinner: 7 Nights.

The Maharajah Bistro and Tandoori
Dinner – 7 days from 6pm
Lunch – Weekends from 11:30am

Takeaways & Deliveries
202 Wellington Ave., Kingsland,
Auckland
Ph 09-555 2233

Port & Starboard seafood bar and grill
**Relaxed dining inside
or outside, overlooking
the harbour. Seafood cuisine.**

6 The Wharf, Auckland City,
Hours: From 11:30am, 7 days
Phone: 09-555 0555
reserve@portstar.co.nz

A **Find the right place for the following situations.**

1. It is 8 o'clock in the morning. Where can you have a cup of coffee?
2. You like Irish music. Where can you go?
3. You would like to take a meal home from a restaurant.
4. You want to go out for dinner with a friend. You both like exotic food.
   Where could you go?

ℹ **am / a.m.** in the morning
(before 12 o'clock)

pm / p.m. in the afternoon /
evening (after 12 o'clock)

B **Look at the adverts in A again.**
Find a restaurant / café you and your partner would both like to go to.

How about Indian?

That's a
good idea!

I love
Indian food.

Shall we go
to a café?

I'd prefer
to go to the pub.

2 What do you expect from a restaurant?

A Read the restaurant review. Find the adjectives and write then in the following categories.

> **Restaurant of the week** by Joanne Lockey
>
> ★ **The Green Star**
>
> The Green Star is a lovely restaurant in Hamilton Street. It has a great atmosphere and the food is delicious. My chicken salad was really tasty and the service was fast and friendly.
>
> All in all, the Green Star is excellent value for money.

Atmosphere	Service	Food	Value for money
great			

B Here are some more words to describe a good or bad restaurant. Write them in the categories in A and add others you know.

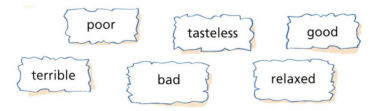

poor   tasteless   good   terrible   bad   relaxed

C Use the words from A and B to write a review of a restaurant you visited recently.

Restaurant Review

_____

_____

_____

_____

83

PORT & STARBOARD
SEAFOOD BAR AND GRILL

Starter
Ham and Melon Mix
Garlic Cheese Bread
Soup of the Day

Main Course
Thai Beef Salad
with sweet chilli - very spicy!

Warm Smoked Salmon
with baked potato, artichokes and onions

Seafood Laksa
with prawns, mussels, and shrimps

Chicken Supreme
with mushrooms

Arabiatta Vegetarian Pasta
with tomatoes, garlic, basil and parmesan

All main courses are served with a side salad.

Dessert
Passionfruit Pannacotta
with kiwifruit and mint sauce

Baked grapefruit

Service is included.

A Find words in the menu for the following food groups.

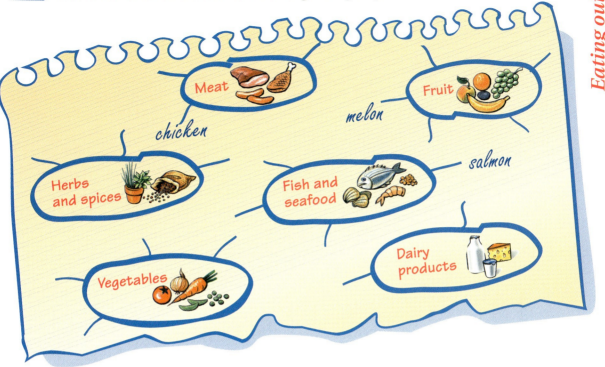

Meat

chicken

Fruit

melon

Herbs and spices

Fish and seafood

salmon

Vegetables

Dairy products

B Group work.
Create your own menu.

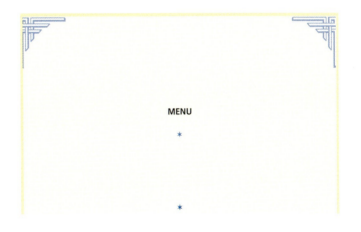

MENU

*

*

Food and Drink Facts

Did you know that Wellington, the capital of New Zealand, has more restaurants, bars and cafés per head than New York? And did you know that New Zealand has over 350 vineyards which produce some of the world's best wines? More than a third of wine produced is exported.

4 Are you ready to order?

A Listen and complete the dialogue.

I'll take   go   do you   I'd like

I'd prefer   have   I'll   can I have

▲ Are you ready to order?

■ Yes, _____ the garlic cheese bread as a starter, and then the seafood Laksa.

▲ I'm sorry, madam, the Laksa is off, but I can recommend the warm smoked salmon, it's very good.

■ Oh, OK, _____ the smoked salmon then, but _____ it _____ with rice instead of the baked potato?

▲ Yes, of course. And you, sir?

● Well, _____ the ham and melon mix as a starter, and then I'll _____ the vegetarian pasta for my main course but without the parmesan, please.

▲ Certainly. And anything else? I can recommend some very good local wines.

● Oh, you don't have any Villa Maria wine, _____?

▲ _____ just _____ and check!

● That would be great.

> **Future: will**
> I'll (will) **take** the ...
> I'll (will) **have** the ...
> I'll (will) just **go** and **check**.
> ➜ page 139

B Role Play. Order a meal in a restaurant. Use you own menu from 3B.

'Excuse me, I ordered the non-sticky menu.'

Quick Quiz

Grammar

Fill in the verb in the correct form.

1. I _____ (have) the smoked salmon.

2. I _____ just _____ and _____ (go, check).

3. I _____ (take) the pasta.

Vocabulary

Find the opposites.

1. ☐☐☐☐☐ – tasteless
2. good – ☐☐☐
3. ☐☐☐☐☐ – terrible
4. excellent – ☐☐☐☐
5. ☐☐☐☐☐☐☐ – unfriendly
6. ☐☐☐☐ – slow

Phrases

Complete the phrases.

1. _____ we go to a café?
2. _____ about Indian?
3. I'd _____the ham and melon mix.
4. I'd _____ the garlic cheese bread.
5. Can I _____ it with rice?
6. And anything _____ ?
7. I can _____ some local wines.

Grammar: 1. Take 2. 'll have 3. 'll 4. Can 5. Shall
Vocabulary: 1.tasty 2. bad 3. great 4. poor 5. friendly 6. fast
Phrases: 1. Shall 2. How 3. prefer/like 4. like/prefer 5. have 6. else 7. recommend

In Unit 10 haben Sie:
- Vorschläge gemacht, in welches Restaurant Sie gerne gehen würden.
- auf Vorschläge reagiert.
- sich auf ein Restaurant geeinigt.
- ein Restaurant empfohlen.
- im Restaurant etwas bestellt.

GRAMMATIK Gr

→ Zukunft mit *will*
→ Frageanhängsel

A **Schreiben Sie die Reaktionen (in Klammern) als ganze Sätze.**

1. It's cold in here! (close the window)

   I'll close the window. _____ .

2. What would you like? (have the chicken)

   I _____ .

3. Which wine would you like? (have the Chianti)

   We_____ .

4. Can someone go to the bank for me? (go)

   Yes, OK. I _____ .

5. Are you meeting me at the station? (be there)

   No, but Kate _____ .

6. I don't think I know how to get there. (show you)

   Don't worry, I _____ .

> **Zukunftsform: will**
> - *Will* wird verwendet, wenn man verspricht, etwas zu tun oder etwas bestellt, z.B. *I'll have the Garlic Cheese Bread*
>   *I'll just go and check.*
> - *Will* bleibt bei allen Personen unverändert. Die Verneinungsform von *will* ist *will not (won't).*

B Vervollständigen Sie die Sätze mit den Wörtern auf den Kärtchen (können mehrfach verwendet werden).

included	served	are	is

1. Breakfast _____ from
   7 am - 11 am.

2. All meals _____ with a side salad.

3. "Happy Hour": cocktails _____
   at half price!

4. Lunch _____ from
   12 pm - 3 pm.

5. A free drink _____ with every
   meal.

6. Service _____.

*'Damn, it's Happy Hour. We'll never get a
drink.'*

Frageanhängsel
- Mit Hilfe eines Frageanhängsel kann man aus einer Aussage eine indirekte Frage machen.
- Bei einem verneinten Zeitwort steht das Anhängsel in der bejahten Form.
- Ist das Zeitwort bejaht, muss das Frageanhängsel in der verneinten Form stehen: *You don't have any Villa Maria wine, **do you**?*

C Ordnen Sie jeder Fragen ein passendes Frageanhängsel zu.

1. You don't have any Australian wine,

2. You like Irish music,

3. They hate fish,

4. You don't like Italian food,

5. He doesn't speak English,

6. She plays tennis very well,

don't they?

doesn't she?

do you?

does he?

don't you?

do you?

D Vervollständigen Sie die Fragen.

Are you

Can I have

How about

Anything

Shall we go

When

Do

What

1. _____ to a restaurant?

2. _____ would you like to eat?

3. _____ you like Indian food?

4. _____ Italian?

5. _____ shall we meet?

6. _____ ready to order?

7. _____ the chicken without mushrooms?

8. _____ else?

E Bringen Sie den Dialog in die richtige Reihenfolge.

▲ That's a good idea!

▲ Come on, let's go! I'm hungry.

● Not always! How about the new Italian restaurant? It's very good value for money.

● You can have pasta then!

▲ What shall we do this evening?

● I went to the cinema yesterday. Why don't we go out for dinner?

▲ Oh yes! The food there's delicious.

▲ _____

■ Let's go to the cinema!

● _____

▲ _____

■ I'd prefer to go to the pub. Restaurants are expensive.

● _____

▲ _____

■ I don't like pizza.

● _____

▲ _____

F **Lösen Sie das Kreuzworträtsel mit Wörtern aus der Speisekarte (S. 40). Aufgepasst! Manche Ziffern kommen waagerecht (*across*) UND senkrecht (*down*) vor.**

Across →

1. You make a sandwich with it.

2. _____ and spices.

4. A kind of seafood.

5. A red fruit. You eat them in salads.

6. A tasty dairy product. France is famous for it.

7. It's red meat.

Down ↓

1. The first meal of the day.

2. You eat this after your main course.

3. You usually eat three _____ every day.

4. _____ course.

5. Fruit and _____ .

6. The first course of a meal.

7. It's white meat.

8. A big fruit

ℹ **Red meat –– white meat**
In englischsprachigen Ländern wird beim Fleisch in *red* und *white meat* unterschieden. Zu *red* meat (dunkel) zählen Lamm und Rind, zu *white* meat (helles Fleisch) Geflügel (*poultry*) oder Kalbsfleisch (*veal*).

Health and body

1 **Body and soul**

A Write the activities from the pictures under the appropriate verb.

play	go	do	eat
_____	*to the gym*	_____	_____
	_____	_____	_____

B Which of the above do you do regularly? What would you like to do that you do not do?

> I eat fish regularly.

> I don't eat much fruit.

> I'd like to go to the gym, but I never have time.

C Pairwork. What do you do to keep fit and healthy? Ask your partner.

> **ⓘ** once a week
> twice a week
> three times a week

D Report something interesting about your partner.

> She does yoga once a week.

> He goes hiking regularly.

2   Health problems

A   Label the body
parts in the cartoon.

66 How am I??? I feel *terrible*. I have a headache, in fact my whole body aches – neck, shoulders, back, arms, legs – *and* I have a sore throat, my nose is running. I think I have flu, or maybe I'm just stressed. Oh, and I broke my foot last week ...99

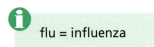

flu = influenza

B   What illnesses can you find in the cartoon? What other common health complaints
do you know?

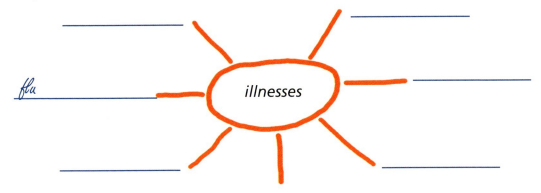

flu

illnesses

C   What should you do when you are ill? Do you have any good remedies/tips?
Tell the class.

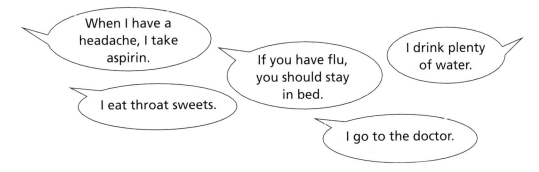

When I have a
headache, I take
aspirin.

If you have flu,
you should stay
in bed.

I drink plenty
of water.

I eat throat sweets.

I go to the doctor.

3 Stress and relaxation

A Complete the text.

More than one in three people report that they are affected by stress. What can you do to reduce stress? Here are a few ways:

● Eat _____ .

● Stop _____ – it doesn't help you to stay healthy, even if you think it relaxes you.

● Don't drink a lot of tea, coffee or other drinks with _____ .

● Don't drink too much _____ – it will make you feel worse!

● Be physically _____ – do sport, it gives you more _____ .

● Talk to family and _____ – they may be able to help you.

● Try relaxation _____ .

smoking

energy

techniques

caffeine

active

friends

healthily

alcohol

Imperative
Try relaxation.
Don't drink a lot of tea.
→ page 145

B Which do you think is the best tip?

C Look at the pictures and read the text. Now listen and try the relaxation technique.

Sit with your back straight.

1. Lift your right leg and point your toes for five seconds, then relax. Repeat with your left leg.

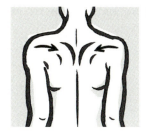

3. Now stand up with your back straight and pull your shoulder blades together for five seconds, then relax.

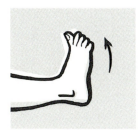

2. Lift your right leg and pull your foot back for five seconds, then relax. Repeat with your left leg.

4. Raise your arms and stretch as high as you can for five seconds.

Now close your eyes. Take a deep breath. Breathe out slowly and open your eyes.

4 Whatever the weather

A **What's your favourite season? Which of the following weather words do you associate with that season?**

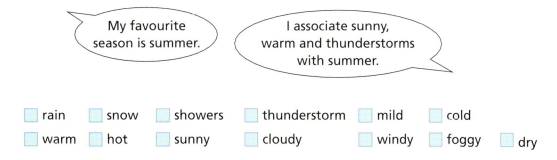

My favourite season is summer.

I associate sunny, warm and thunderstorms with summer.

☐ rain ☐ snow ☐ showers ☐ thunderstorm ☐ mild ☐ cold
☐ warm ☐ hot ☐ sunny ☐ cloudy ☐ windy ☐ foggy ☐ dry

B Which of the following clothes do you *normally* associate with each season? Add others.

shorts	gloves	warm boots	_____
dress	skirt	coat	_____
sandals	scarf	_____	

C Listen to the weekly weather report. Match the weather to the days. Then report.

sunshine and showers

hot and sunny periods

cloudy and windy

rain

sunny and warm

thunderstorms

Monday _____

Tuesday _____

Wednesday _____

Thursday _____

Friday _____

Saturday _____

Sunday _____

Monday and Tuesday will be sunny and warm.

There'll be sunshine and showers on Wednesday.

> **Future: *will***
> Monday **will be** sunny and warm.
> → page 139

D Pairwork. Discuss your plans for the weekend with a partner.

What will you do ...

... if it rains?
... if it's sunny?
... if it's cold and foggy?

... if it's hot?
... if it snows?

> **Conditional with *will***
> If it**'s** sunny, I**'ll go** hiking.
> If it **rains**, I **won't play** tennis.
> → page 140

I think I'll go hiking if it's sunny.

If it rains, I won't play tennis.

Health and body

Quick Quiz

Grammar

Put in the verbs in the correct form.

1. _____ (eat) healthily.

2. _____ (be) physically active.

3. _____ (not drink) too much alcohol.

4. Monday and Tuesday _____ (be) sunny and warm.

5. There _____ (be) sunshine and showers on Wednesday.

6. If it _____ (rain), I_____ (stay) at home.

Vocabulary

Match the words with the correct ending.

| ache | ed | ly | ily | ache | ly |

1. health_____

2. head_____

3. physical_____

4. back_____

5. stress_____

6. regular_____

Phrases

Put the phrases in order.

1. goes • gym • week • he • the • twice • to • a

   _____

2. regularly • eat • I • fish

   _____

3. once • she • yoga • a • does • week

   _____

Grammar: 1. Eat 2. Be 3. Don't drink 4. will be 5. 'll be 6. rains, 'll stay

Vocabulary: 1. healthily 2. headache 3. physically 4. backache 5. stressed 6. regularly

Phrases: 1. He goes to the gym twice a week. 2. I eat fish regularly. 3. She does yoga once a week.

In **Unit 11** haben Sie:
- darüber gesprochen, was Sie tun um gesund und fit zu bleiben.
- jemandem Ratschläge gegeben, der sich nicht wohl fühlt.
- eine Entspannungsübung nach Anleitung ausgeführt.
- den Wetterbericht verstanden und besprochen, was Sie – je nach Wetter – unternehmen werden.

GRAMMATIK GRAMMAT

→ *will* für Vorhersagen
→ Befehlsform
→ Bedingungssätze mit *will*

A Markieren Sie die sechs versteckten Wörter. Sie haben alle etwas mit Krankheit zu tun.

K	F	B	H	T	O	I	Z	O	I	U	O
K	N	P	G	B	I	L	L	I	Z	S	O
B	G	K	A	D	E	C	H	T	G	O	E
B	I	U	O	C	S	V	H	O	R	R	L
D	H	E	A	D	A	C	H	E	H	E	P
T	G	I	A	T	I	U	O	S	G	T	N
P	H	B	O	S	N	O	R	U	F	T	V
H	F	A	G	T	E	F	R	J	I	H	I
O	N	C	R	N	O	L	T	C	U	R	O
R	P	K	W	E	X	U	N	T	O	O	S
D	I	A	O	E	Q	K	F	B	H	A	O
W	Z	C	C	U	O	R	D	R	P	T	M
E	X	H	N	H	O	I	S	D	I	U	O
E	Q	E	F	S	T	R	E	S	S	E	D

B Ordnen Sie die Satzanfänge und Satzenden richtig zu.

1. When you're stressed

2. When I have a cold

3. When I have backache

4. When I have flu

5. When I do sport

6. If you think you have broken your arm

I go swimming.

you should go to hospital.

I normally stay in bed.

I drink plenty of tea.

you should try yoga.

I feel good.

*I don't drink coffee for breakfast.
I think it's unhealthy.*

C Was würden sie jemandem raten, der besonders <u>ungesund</u> leben möchte.
Bilden Sie Sätze.

1. eat a lot of fruit
2. smoke a lot
3. drink plenty of coffee

4. do sport
5. go hiking
6. watch plenty of television

Dos and Don'ts for an Unhealthy Lifestyle

1. _____.

2. _____.

3. _____.

4. _____.

5. _____.

6. _____.

D Tragen Sie neben jedem Wetterwort die Nummer des passenden Wettersymbols ein.

1 ☀ 2 🌧 3 🌥 4 ☁ 5 🌦 6 ⛈

sunny and showers ☐   cloudy ☐   sunny periods ☐

sunny ☐   thunderstorms ☐   rain ☐

E Vervollständigen Sie den Wetterbericht.

sunny

will be

will have

periods   showers

there'll be sunshine

cloudy   it'll be

there'll be rain

thunderstorms

(Map of Europe with weather symbols:)
Helsinki
Oslo   Stockholm
Edinburgh
Dublin
London   Berlin
Brussels   Prague
Paris   Vienna
Budapest
Constanta
Madrid   Rome 26°C
Lisboa
Athens 32°C

❝ ... and here's the weather forecast for European cities. In Athens _____ hot and sunny with temperatures around 32°C. Rome _____ a little cooler with 26°C, but _____ all day. Lisbon _____ some _____ , followed by sunny _____. In Berlin _____. London will start _____ with sunny periods later, while Brussels will enjoy some sunshine in the morning, but it'll be cloudy in the afternoon. In Dublin _____. Finally, in Paris there'll be _____ after a very hot day with temperatures around 30°C. ❞

Zukunft mit *will*

- Mit ***will*** kann man auch eine **Vorhersage** formulieren, z.B.
  There'll be sunshine and showers on Wednesday.

- ***Will*** wird außerdem verwendet, wenn man etwas **verspricht** oder im
  Restaurant **bestellt** (siehe Unit 10), z.B. *I'll just go and check* oder *I'll
  have the garlic cheese bread.*

F **Vervollständigen Sie die Bedingungssätze mit den Wörtern / Satzteilen auf den
Kärtchen.**

> be healthier

> call you next week

> buy the drinks

> go cycling

> come and see you

1. If you give me your phone number, I *'ll* _____.

2. If I have time on Saturday, I _____.

3. If you eat plenty of fresh fruit and vegetables, you _____.

4. If it's sunny next weekend, we _____.

5. If you organize the food, I _____.

Bedingungssätze mit *will*
Bedingungssätze bestehen aus einer Bedingung und einer Folge.
Bedingung: If + Zeitwort im Present Simple, z.B. *If it's sunny*,
Folge: will + Grundform des Zeitworts, z.B. *I'll go hiking.*

G **Nummerieren Sie die Körperteile.**

leg ☐

shoulder ☐

ear ☐

fingers ☐

neck ☐

mouth ☐

foot ☐

arm ☐

knee ☐

nose ☐

head ☐

eye ☐

Revision

A What is it?

1. Choose three words to describe a place, person or object.
2. Write the three words on the board.
3. The others guess what the words describe.

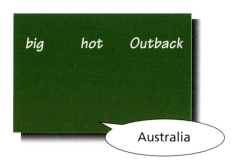

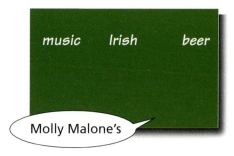

B Quick replies

1. With a partner make as many phrases/questions as you can.

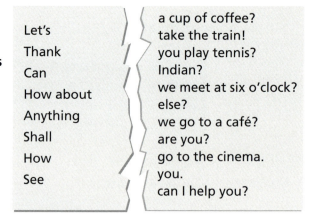

Let's	a cup of coffee?
Thank	take the train!
Can	you play tennis?
How about	Indian?
	we meet at six o'clock?
Anything	else?
Shall	we go to a café?
How	are you?
See	go to the cinema.
	you.
	can I help you?

2. Now stand in a circle. Throw a ball to someone else in the circle and say one of your phrases.
3. The person who catches the ball replies.
4. Continue until everyone has spoken.

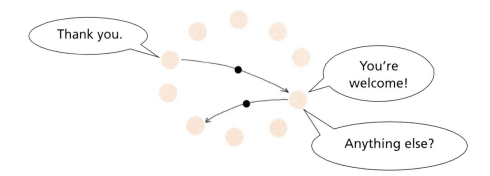

C **What's your problem**

1. Write a simple health problem on a piece of paper.
2. Stick the paper on the back
   of a person in the group.

headache

3. The others read your problem and give you advice.
4. Guess what problem you have from the advice the others give you.

How about
a head massage?

You should drink
plenty of water.

Why don't you
take an aspirin?

 D **"Simon says"**

Listen and play "Simon says".
There is only one rule: Only do the things that begin with "Simon says ...". If you do
any of the other things, you are out of the game.

E **Conditional sentences**

1. Write a sentence beginning with *If* on a piece of paper. Then pass the paper to the
   person on your left.

   If it rains,

2. Complete your neighbour's sentence. Then pass the paper to the person on your
   left.

   If it rains, I will stay at home.

3. Start a new sentence starter under the first one. Pass the paper to the person on
   your left.

   If it rains, I will stay at home.
   If I stay at home,

4. Continue writing and completing sentences until you get your own paper back.
5. Now read out your sentences to the group.

Places

1 Where do you live?

A Look at the photographs and tick the correct word.

in the ☐ country ☐ mountains

in a ☐ city ☐ village

on a ☐ hill ☐ farm

by the ☐ river ☐ sea

near the ☐ airport ☐ station

B Read the text and find the name of the village on the map.

66 I live in a small village in the country. It's about 35 kilometres north-east of Dartmouth, which is the nearest city. I live quite a long way from the sea. My village is near the airport on route 2.99

This person lives in

_____ .

C Describe where you live.

I live ...

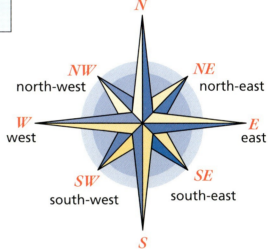

D Where's your favourite place to sit at home?

I have a comfortable chair by the window.

2 How do I get there?

P + R

Avoid the traffic jams – take the tube

See Piccadilly Circus in a new light - get on a double decker!

Discover London by underground

"Change here for Madame"

Take it easy, take the train into the heart of London.

With the Day Travelcard you can visit the Tate Gallery, the Houses of Parliament and still go shopping at Harrod's. Get on and off the bus as often as you want all day.

ⓘ tube = London underground

A Find the names of London tourist attractions above and then locate them on the map below.

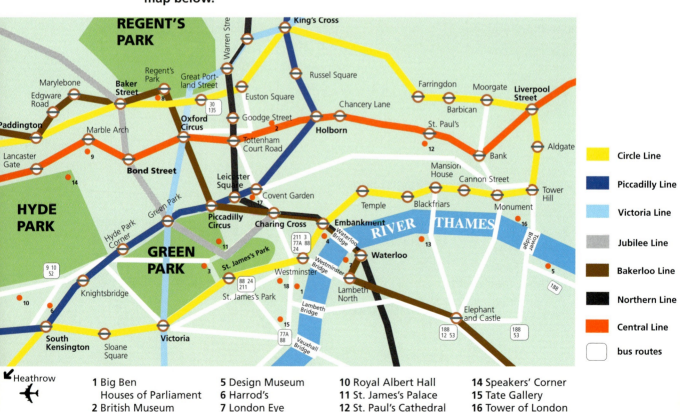

Circle Line
Piccadilly Line
Victoria Line
Jubilee Line
Bakerloo Line
Northern Line
Central Line
bus routes

1 Big Ben
Houses of Parliament
2 British Museum
3 Buckingham Palace
4 Cleopatra's Needle

5 Design Museum
6 Harrod's
7 London Eye
8 Madame Tussaud's
9 Marble Arch

10 Royal Albert Hall
11 St. James's Palace
12 St. Paul's Cathedral
13 Shakespeare Globe
Theatre & Museum

14 Speakers' Corner
15 Tate Gallery
16 Tower of London
17 Trafalgar Square
18 Westminster Abbey

B **Listen to the dialogue and answer the following questions.**

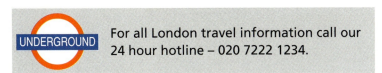

UNDERGROUND   For all London travel information call our
24 hour hotline – 020 7222 1234.

1. Where is the caller? _____

2. Where does the caller want to go? _____

 C **Listen to the dialogue again and complete the note.**

Take the P_____ Line into
L_____. Change to the _____ Line.
Get off at W_____. Take the _____
bus, travelling towards L_____ Bridge.

D **Role play. Choose a tourist attraction on the map and tell your partner how to get there.**

Excuse me,
can you tell me
how to get to …?

3   Lost and found

 A **Match the problems and the advice. Then listen and check.**

1. Excuse me. I've left my umbrella on the underground. Can you help me?   [ ]

2. Oh no. I don't have any change for the ticket machine.   [ ]

3. Hello. Can you help me, please? Someone has stolen my purse.   [ ]

A Oh dear, I'm sorry. You should go to the police.

B Have you asked in the lost property office?

C Don't worry. You can use your debit card instead.

B **Brainstorm other things you can forget or get stolen.**

C **Role play. Choose a problem and ask for advice.**

4 Changes

A Read the letter and underline the things that have changed.

Dear Kath,
                                    Sunderland, 25th May
I'm sorry I haven't written to you sooner, but I've been so busy since I came back to Sunderland to visit my family. So much has changed since we were at school here, it's unbelievable. They've finished the new metro line now which takes you from the airport directly into the city. The Queen opened it as part of her Golden Jubilee Tour! Do you remember how long it took when we were last here? The shopping centre has changed a lot, too. They've built a roof over the whole high street, it really was like a wind tunnel before.

Yesterday I walked along the river for the first time in years. They've built new paths for walkers and cyclists along the river and artists have created sculptures and pictures about the history of the area - it's really interesting.
The city has changed a lot since we lived here, but there are still some of the old places, like Fitzers, the coffee shop we went to after school - that hasn't changed at all.

I'm sending you some photos and hope to write again soon.
Take care,
Julia

Present Perfect	**Past Simple**
They've **finished** the new metro line.	Yesterday I **walked** along the river

→ page 139

B Are the following statements true or false?

	true	false
1. Kath and Julia didn't travel on the new metro when they last visited Sunderland.	☐	☐
2. The high street is like a wind tunnel since they built a roof.	☐	☐
3. Kath has walked along the river for years.	☐	☐
4. Fitzers coffee shop has changed a lot.	☐	☐

C Imagine you are writing to a friend who has moved away from your home town. Describe what has changed.

Bridges

A new tourist attraction near Sunderland in North-East England is the Gateshead Millennium Bridge which crosses the River Tyne. It is also called the "Blinking Eye" because when it moves up to let ships pass under, it looks like an eye closing and opening.

Gateshead Millennium Bridge

Quick Quiz

Grammar

Past Simple or *Present Perfect*. **Put the verbs in the correct tense.**

1. Someone _____ (steal) my purse.

2. I _____ (be) so busy since I _____ (come) back to Sunderland.

3. So much _____ (change) since we _____ (be) at school here.

4. They _____ (build) a roof over the high street, it really _____ (be) like a wind tunnel before.

5. Yesterday I _____ (walk) along the river for the first time in years.

Vocabulary

Fill in the missing prepositions.

1. I live _____ a small village.

2. My house is a long way _____ the sea.

3. It is north-east _____ Dartmouth.

4. Discover London _____ underground.

5. Get _____ the bus at Waterloo and take the tube.

6. I've left my umbrella _____ the underground.

Phrases

Find the last word of each phrase.

1. Excuse _____.

2. Oh dear, I'm _____.

3. Don't _____.

4. Take _____.

In Unit 13 haben Sie:
- die Lage Ihres Wohnortes näher beschrieben.
- nach den Verkehrsverbindungen zu einem bestimmten Ziel in einer Stadt gefragt.
- beschrieben, wie man in einer Stadt mit öffentlichen Verkehrsmitteln an einen gewünschten Ort kommt.
- ein Problem geschildert und bei der Lösung eines Problems geholfen.
- in einem Brief beschrieben, was sich in Ihrer Stadt im Vergleich zu früher verändert hat.

GRAMMATIK GRAMMATIK (

➡ Present Perfect
➡ Present Perfect und Past Simple

A Setzen Sie die fehlenden Verhältniswörter ein.
(Manche können auch mehrfach verwendet werden).

from	on	of	in	by	near

1. **"**I live _____ a farm _____ Sweden. It's about five kilometres south _____ a small town called Sorsele. Our farm is near the mountains, but a long way _____ the sea.**"**

2. **"**We live in a big city _____ the sea. We live in a flat _____ the city centre, so we are near the shops and the school. It's about five minutes to the nearest underground station, but we live a long way _____ the airport.**"**

B In den folgenden Sätzen kommt jeweils das Zeitwort *get* in Kombination mit einem Verhältniswort vor. Ergänzen Sie die Sätze mit den richtigen Übersetzungen.

| on | to | off | around | on |

1. Take bus no. 77A and *get* _____ at Westminster. (aussteigen)

2. Excuse me, how do I _____ the Odeon cinema? (kommen)

3. Change at Victoria Station and _____ the Gatwick Express. (einsteigen)

4. I live in a small town, so I can _____ easily by bike. (herumkommen)

5. She likes her job, and she _____ very well with her colleagues. (zurechtkommen)

C Was wurde in der Stadt verändert? Was wurde nicht verändert?

1. ✔ finish the new underground line

2.   open a new shopping centre

3.   build a new indoor swimming pool

4. ✔ create a new industrial area outside the town centre

5. ✔ renovate a lot of the historical buildings in town

6. ✔ open a few new restaurants

7.   move the post office to the station

1. *They've* _____.
2. *They haven't* _____.
3. _____.
4. _____.
5. _____.
6. _____.
7. _____.

> **Present Perfect oder Past Simple?**
> • Das Present Perfect wird oft verwendet, wenn allgemein etwas berichtet wird, z.B. *They've finished the new metro line.*
>   Entscheidend ist das Ereignis selbst, nicht wann oder wie es passiert ist.
>
> • Werden zu einem Ereignis Zeitangaben gemacht, dann verwendet man in der Regel das Past Simple: *The Queen opened it (the new metro line) as part of her Golden Jubilee Tour.*

D *Present Perfect* oder *Past Simple*? Setzen Sie die Zeitwörter in der richtigen Form ein.

| find | enclose | have | say | not write |

| start | be | move |

Dear Jonathan,

I'm sorry I _____ for so long, but we

_____ a very busy year!

I think I _____ last year that we were looking for a

new house and we finally _____ one in May and

_____ in August. So we now live in Shrewsbury not

far from Nick's new office. He _____ his new job in

April and loves it. The house itself is quite small, but has a big garden

which will be very useful next summer because our daughter, Emily, was

born in February! She's great! That _____ the

biggest change this year. I _____ some photos of

our new daughter and new home – you should come and see us in the

New Year!

Have a great Christmas!

Love,

Melissa

E *Since* oder *for*? Setzen Sie ein.

1. They've built three new blocks of flats _____ 2001.

2. They haven't renovated the school _____ more than twenty years.

3. We haven't seen each other _____ we graduated from university.

4. I haven't been back to Canada _____ six years.

5. Brian has been my boss _____ 1997.

6. She's been ill _____ Sunday.

> **For oder since?**
> • **For** steht vor einer Zeitangabe, die einen Zeitraum beschreibt, z.B.
>   **for the first time in years** (zum ersten Mal seit Jahren).
> • **Since** steht vor einer Zeitangabe, die sich auf einen Zeitpunkt bezieht,
>   z.B. **since we were at school** (seit wir in der Schule waren).

F Lesen Sie die Sätze und kreuzen sie die richtige deutsche Übersetzung an.

1. They have lived here for two years.

☐ Sie haben zwei Jahre hier gelebt.

☐ Sie leben seit zwei Jahren hier.

2. She has not used her credit card for three months.

☐ Sie hat seit drei Monaten ihre Kreditkarte nicht mehr benutzt.

☐ Sie benutzte Ihre Kreditkarte drei Monate lang nicht.

3. Stephen has worked there for five years.

☐ Stephen hat fünf Jahre dort gearbeitet.

☐ Stephen arbeitet seit fünf Jahren dort.

G Welche Wörter passen zusammen? Bilden Sie Wortpaare.

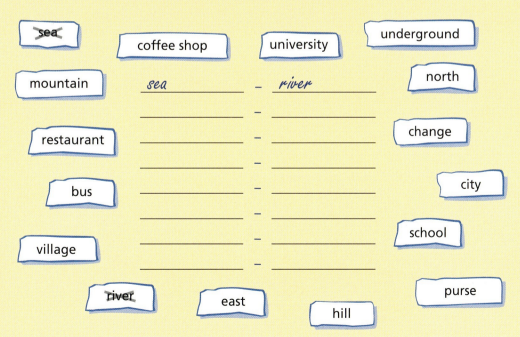

sea ~~~   coffee shop   university   underground

mountain   *sea* – *river*   north

restaurant   _____ – _____

   _____ – _____   change

bus   _____ – _____   city

   _____ – _____

village   _____ – _____   school

   _____ – _____

river ~~~   east   hill   purse

Shopping

Classifieds

FREE PET SKUNK with purchase of cage for $250. House-trained, 6 months, friendly. 320-555-3130

'02 FORD FOCUS sporty, fun, low mileage. $9,997 494 Lyndale 952-555-2271

Groceries Online
- ☐ Home
- ☐ Our Food
- ☐ Healthy Eating
- ☐ This Weeks Offers

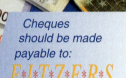

Cheques should be made payable to:
F*I*T*Z*E*R*S

1   Where do you shop?

A   Add extra items to the table below and compare with a partner.

What things would you buy ...

in a shop	on the internet	from a catalogue	from a newspaper
bread	*cheap flights*	*clothes*	*second-hand car*

> I buy food in a supermarket.

> I don't buy anything on the internet.

> I sometimes order clothes from a catalogue.

B   How would you pay for the items in A?

> I use cash to buy food.

> I always use my credit card on the internet.

ℹ️ I pay cash.
I pay **by** — credit card.
— debit card.
— cheque.

2 In the shop

A **Customer or sales assistant. Who says what?**

	customer	sales assistant
1. Is that all?	☐	☐
2. How much is it?	☐	☐
3. Do you accept cheques?	☐	☐
4. Could you wrap it, please?	☐	☐
5. Do you have a store card?	☐	☐
6. How would you like to pay?	☐	☐
7. Would you sign here, please?	☐	☐
8. I'm just looking, thanks.	☐	☐

B **Pronunciation. Listen and practise the phrases in A.**

C **Listen to the dialogue and tick what you hear.**

■ Do you have any black gloves?

▲ Just let me check for you. No I'm sorry, we don't have any in black, but we have some in blue.

■ No that's OK, thank you. I'll just take the ☐ scarf / ☐ gloves / ☐ hat .

▲ OK. Is that all?

■ Yes. How much is it?

▲ That's ☐ 19.99 / ☐ 29.99 / ☐ 9.99. Do you have a store card?

■ No, I don't.

▲ How would you like to pay?

■ By ☐ cheque / ☐ credit card / ☐ debit card, please.

▲ Would you sign here, please? ... Here's your receipt. Thank you very much.

■ Thank you. Goodbye.

▲ Bye.

> **Some / any**
> Do you have **any** black gloves?
> We don't have **any** in black.
> We have **some** in blue. ➔ page 142

D **Role play. Buy something. One of you is the shop assistant, the other is the customer.**

3 Online shopping

A Look at the internet page and fill in the order form for one of the products.

Present passive
This beautiful coffee table **is made** of wood.
Only top quality materials **are used**.
→ page 139

B **Listen to the dialogue. What's the problem?**

■ Good morning, Home Comforts, can I help you?

▲ Good morning, I'd like to speak to someone in the customer services department, please.

■ One moment please, I'll put you through.

● Good morning, customer services.

▲ Oh hello, I'm calling about a coffee table I ordered from you recently.

☐ The table hasn't arrived.

☐ They delivered the wrong one.

☐ The glass top is broken.

C **Match the beginnings and endings of the telephone phrases below.**

I'll put you	hold?
I'm sorry, the	call back later.
Would you like to	line is busy.
No thank you, I'll	through.

D **Role play. Choose one of the other problems in B and call customer services.**

What do we buy online?

Two thirds, or 66%, of internet users worldwide have bought products online. In Germany, the UK and the US more than three quarters of internet users shop online. But what do they buy? Books, CDs and computer equipment are still the most popular things to buy online. However, online shoppers also like to buy tickets or make reservations, buy videos and DVDs, and health and beauty products. Clothes are not so popular because they like to try them on first.

And why don't the other 33% of internet users shop online? Some don't shop online because they don't want to pay for delivery. They are also often worried about security and don't want to pay by credit card.

4 High-tech lives

A Read the article. What does the author use her computer for?

The Modern Hermit

Working from home has changed my life. I used to go out regularly with friends and chat with the neighbours. I even went to the office. I used to spend so much time commuting to work. Now I don't have to worry about traffic jams. I never need to leave home. With my computer I can work, shop and chat with all kinds of people in my home office. It's fantastic!

Stress is no longer a problem. My biggest worry in the morning is which newspaper to read while I'm having breakfast. There are so many to choose from: *The New York Times, The Independent, The Sydney Morning Herald* for example. I don't usually like sport, but surfing is now my favourite hobby. I have to limit myself so that I can get other things done.

Life has never been better. Banking and shopping for groceries are two things I hate. However, I've found doing them online much more agreeable. I don't have to wait in queues and my food is delivered to my door. I have become a modern hermit. Except I am not alone. You can never be alone in cyber space. Somebody somewhere is always online and happy to chat.

I might leave the house one day, but right now I'm in no hurry.

- ☐ online banking
- ☐ plan holidays
- ☐ e-mail
- ☐ shop
- ☐ meet people / make friends
- ☐ read the newspaper
- ☐ surf
- ☐ play games
- ☐ look for jobs
- ☐ chat
- ☐ work

B Would you want to be a "modern hermit"? Why? Why not?

C What do you use a computer for? Has it changed your life?

Quick Quiz

Grammar

Underline the correct word.

1. I have some/any money.
2. I don't have some/any credit cards.
3. Do you have some/any black gloves.

4. This is/has made of wood.
5. Only the best quality materials are/have used.

Vocabulary

Complete the nouns.

1. ☐ n t ☐ r n ☐ t
2. c r ☐ d ☐ t c ☐ r d
3. s t ☐ r ☐ c ☐ r d
4. c h ☐ q ☐ ☐
5. d ☐ l ☐ v ☐ r
6. ☐ - m ☐ ☐ l
7. h ☐ m ☐ ☐ f f ☐ c ☐
8. c ☐ m p ☐ t ☐ r

Phrases

Complete the shopping phrases.

1. Is that _____?
2. Do you _____ cheques?
3. Could you _____ it, please?
4. _____ would you like to pay?
5. I'm just _____.

Phrases: 1. all 2. accept 3. wrap 4. How 5. looking

Vocabulary: 1. internet 2. credit card 3. store card 4. cheque 5. delivery 6. e-mail 7. home office 8. computer

Grammar: 1. some 2. any 3. any 4. is 5. are

119

In Unit 14 haben Sie:
- über Ihre Einkaufsgewohnheiten gesprochen.
- in einem Geschäft nach etwas gefragt.
- eine Internet-Bestellung ausgefüllt.
- ein kurzes Telefongespräch geführt.
- über Verwendungsmöglichkeiten für Computer gesprochen.

GRAMMATIK GE

➜ *Some* und *any*
➜ Present passive

A *Some* oder *any*? Setzen Sie ein.

1. ▲ Can you recommend _____ good restaurants here in town?

   ■ Yes, there are quite a few in the centre, but _____ of them are very expensive.

2. ● Do you have _____ blue T-shirts?

   ▲ No, I'm sorry, we don't have _____ in blue, but we have _____ in black or red.

3. I'd like _____ of those apples over there, please.

4. You don't have _____ Australian red wine, do you?

5. _____ people don't shop online because they don't want to pay for delivery.

6. I don't have _____ change for the ticket machine.

> **Some oder any?**
> - **Some** wird in der Regel bei bejahten Aussagen verwendet:
>   *We have **some** in blue.*
>
> - **Any** wird bei Fragen und verneinten Aussagen verwendet:
>   *Do you have **any** black gloves?*
>   *No, I'm sorry, we don't have **any** in black.*

B Ergänzen Sie die unvollständigen Wörter mit *some* oder *any*.

1. I don't buy _____*thing*__ on the internet.

2. _____*body*_____*where* is always online and happy to chat.

3. I know _____*one* who buys almost everthing second-hand.

4. I haven't bought _____*thing* for my son's birthday yet.

5. I have to buy _____ *thing* for my mother's birthday.

6. I'd like to speak to _____ *one* in the customer services department.

7. Did you meet _____ *one* you know when you went shopping today?

8. Would you like _____ *thing* else?

C   **Schreiben Sie die Sätze in die Passiv-Form um.**

1. We use only top quality materials.

   Only _____ .

2. We make all our tables to the highest standards.

   All our _____ .

3. We sell these tables all over the world.

   These _____ .

4. We guarantee your satisfaction.

   Your satisfaction _____ .

5. We serve all our main courses with a side salad.

   All our _____ .

6. We make most reservations online.

   Most _____ .

Das Passiv

Wie im Deutschen haben die Zeitwörter im Englischen Aktiv- und Passivformen.
Die Passiv-Form wird mit Hilfe des Partizip Perfekts (*Past Participle*) gebildet.
Dabei wird die entsprechende Form von *to be* vorangestellt.

   Aktiv: *We use only the best quality materials.*
   Passiv: *Only the best quality materials **are used**.*

Die Partizip Perfekt-Form der unregelmäßigen Zeitwörter finden Sie auf S. 146.

D **Setzen Sie die Verhältniswörter ein.**

1. I buy my food _____ a supermarket.

2. Sometimes I buy things _____ a catalogue.

3. I often buy things _____ the internet.

4. Sorry, we don't have any shoes _____ red.

5. Our products are made _____ the highest standards.

6. I'd like to speak _____ someone in the customer services department.

7. We don't accept cheques, but you can pay _____ credit card.

ℹ **Have oder *have got*?**
Sicher ist Ihnen schon das Zeitwort *have got* (dt. haben, besitzen) aufgefallen. *Have got* bedeutet dasselbe wie *have* und wird überwiegend in Großbritannien verwendet.
> We **have** some in blue.   =   We**'ve got** some in blue.
Immer häufiger wird heute *have* verwendet.

Besonderheit: Die Verneinung von *have got* wird mit *not* gebildet. Fragen werden wie bei den Modalverben durch Umkehren von Fürwort und Zeitwort gebildet.
> We **haven't got** any in black.
> **Have** you **got** any black gloves?

E **Kreuzen Sie die jeweils höflichere Variante an.**

1. ☐ Good morning. What do you want?
   ☐ Good morning. Can I help you?

2. ☐ I want a kilo of apples.
   ☐ I'd like a kilo of apples, please.

3. Do you have any black scarves?

   ☐ No.

   ☐ No, I'm sorry, we don't have any in black.

4. ☐ Sign here.

   ☐ Would you sign here, please.

5. Can I help you?

   ☐ No.

   ☐ I'm just looking, thanks.

F Finden Sie das Wort, das nicht in die Reihe passt, und markieren Sie es.

1.	credit card	debit card	cash	cheque	store card
2.	scarf	gloves	hat	coat	pullover
3.	wood	glass	metal	newspaper	plastic
4.	computer	modem	telephone	e-mail	internet

G Bringen Sie die Sätze in die richtige Reihenfolge.

1. to someone • I'd like • customer services department • to speak • please • in the

_____ , _____

_____ .

2. you • moment • through • please • I'll • One • put

_____ , _____ , _____ .

3. busy • sorry • the • I'm • line's.

_____ , _____ .

4. you • like • to • Would • hold

_____ ?

5. a reservation • I'm • about • last week • I made • calling

_____

_____ .

Party time

1 Invitations

A What would you wear?
Write the type of party under the pictures.

T-shirt

swimming costume

shorts

fancy dress costume

tie

suit

evening suit

evening dress

house-warming party

Halloween party

birthday party

dinner dance

beach barbecue

fancy dress party

leaving party

At a beach barbecue, I'd wear a T-shirt and shorts.

B   **Read the invitations and find the expressions which mean**

❝ we would like to invite you to❞

    formal: _____

    informal: _____

❝please reply❞ _____

**The Directors of SMP
request the pleasure of the company of**

DR. M. MUSE AND PARTNER

at the opening of their new Montreal branch
1771 Islington Avenue on Friday 15th November at 7:30 p.m.

R.S.V.P.

R.S.V.P. = Répondez s'il vous plaît
→ please say if you can come

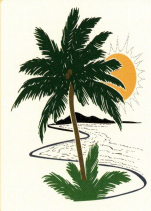

Beach Barbecue

Dear Neighbours,

Let's party! Come along and meet new and old neighbours on Saturday, 24th July from 4pm at the community beach.

Bring a friend   Bring a bottle

to the best beach barbecue of the year.

swimming
sandcastle competition

See you there!
Chris   **beach volleyball**

C   **Brainstorm other types of parties. Have you been to one recently?
Are you going to one soon?**

> I'm going
> to a wedding next
> month.

> I went to
> a fancy dress party
> last Saturday.

D   **Choose a party and write an invitation with a partner.**

2 Doing the right thing

A What advice would you give?

1. *"I'm going to a dinner dance at the weekend, what should I wear?"*

   If I were you …
   - (a) I'd wear casual clothes.
   - (b) I'd wear my favourite outfit.
   - (c) I'd wear something formal like an evening dress.
   - (d) Other: _____

2. *"I'm going to a house-warming party tonight, what shall I take?*

   If I were you …
   - (a) I'd take a bottle of wine.
   - (b) I'd take flowers.
   - (c) I wouldn't take anything.
   - (d) Other: _____

3. *"The party starts at 8 o'clock. What time should I get there?"*

   If I were you …
   - (a) I'd arrive at 8 o'clock.
   - (b) I'd arrive a few minutes to 8.
   - (c) I'd arrive any time before 8:30.
   - (d) Other: _____

4. *"How should I reply to this wedding invitation?"*

   If I were you …
   - (a) I'd phone to say I can come.
   - (b) I'd send a written reply.
   - (c) I'd just go.
   - (d) Other: _____

5. *"I'm going to a cocktail party. Should I eat something before I go?"*

   If I were you …
   - (a) I wouldn't eat anything.
   - (b) I'd have a small snack.
   - (c) I'd have my normal evening meal.
   - (d) Other: _____

> **Conditional with *would***
> If I **were** you, I**'d take** flowers.
> → page 141

B Pairwork. Compare and discuss your answers with a partner.

3 **Small talk**

A **Read the letters and discuss. Do you find the reply helpful?**

Dear Ms Party Perfect,
I often have to socialise with customers in my job and I have a problem with small talk. What can I say? My colleagues, who can talk easily, always enjoy themselves, but I sit on my own in a corner and never know what to say. Can you help me?
Mr Silent

Dear Mr Silent,
It is difficult to make small talk, but you can learn. Before you go out with your customers think of some things to talk about. For example, a new film or book, something interesting about the place you are going to, or something interesting about yourself. Then think of questions to open up the topics you have thought about, for example, "have you seen …", or "did you know …". Small talk is about knowing the right questions to ask and then being interested in the answers. These are just a few ideas which will hopefully help you. Good luck!
Ms Party Perfect

ⓘ a person **who**
a thing **which**

B **Pairwork. Match the following small talk starters with an appropriate reaction.**

1. Have you seen the latest Steven Spielberg film?
2. Did you know that this area is famous for its cheese?
3. Have you met the new managing director yet?
4. What a wonderful dress!
5. What do you think about our latest product?
6. It's a beautiful day today, isn't it?

☐ Thank you very much.

☐ Yes, hopefully it'll be nice at the weekend.

☐ I think it's great.

☐ No, I haven't. Is it good?

☐ No, not yet. What's she like?

☐ Oh really? How interesting.

C **Listen and check.**

D **Do you think the following are acceptable small talk topics?**

☐ the weather   ☐ sport   ☐ health

☐ money / your salary   ☐ politics   ☐ religion

☐ your family   ☐ music   ☐ travel

☐ your hobbies   ☐ your job   ☐ the economy

Think of some small talk topics with a partner and complete the following sentences.

Have you seen _____?

Did you know_____?

What do you think about _____?

F Now practise.

4 A thank-you letter

A Complete the thank-you letter with the following words / phrases.

| hope we shall see each other again soon | met a lot of interesting people | Thank you | kind invitation |

| wonderful party | delicious | Very best wishes | food | kind of you to think of me |

| Dear |

_____ Mary,

_____ for your _____.

It was a _____. The _____ was

_____. We _____

_____. It was very _____

_____.

/ _____.

_____

Janet

Quick Quiz

Grammar

Match the beginnings of the sentences with the appropriate endings.

1. If I were you,   who can talk easily.

2. There are colleagues   which will hopefully help you.

3. These are a few ideas   I'd wear casual clothes.

Vocabulary

Unjumble the words. They are all parties.

1. shoeu gramwin   ☐☐☐☐☐ - ☐☐☐☐☐☐☐
2. windged   ☐☐☐☐☐☐☐
3. tocklaic typar   ☐☐☐☐☐☐☐ ☐☐☐☐☐
4. dreinn deanc   ☐☐☐☐☐☐ ☐☐☐☐☐
5. weenollHa   ☐☐☐☐☐☐☐☐☐
6. rabbucee   ☐☐☐☐☐☐☐☐
7. thirdayb typar   ☐☐☐☐☐☐☐☐ ☐☐☐☐☐

Phrases

Complete the following phrases from this unit.

1. _____ you there.
2. Good _____!
3. It's a beautiful day today, _____ it?
4. Thank you very _____.
5. Oh really? _____ interesting.
6. _____ a wonderful dress!

In Unit 15 haben Sie:
- über verschiedene Arten von Partys gesprochen.
- Einladungen gelesen und selbst eine Einladung geschrieben.
- Ratschläge zum Thema Partys und Einladungen gegeben.
- Über *Small Talk* gesprochen.
- *Small Talk* geübt.
- einen Brief an Ihre Gastgeber geschrieben, um sich zu bedanken.

GRAMMATIK GRAMMATIK GRAMMATIK

→ Bedingungssätze mit *would*
→ Bezügliche Fürwörter *who* und *which*

A Welche sechs Begriffe lassen sich hier zusammensetzen.
Sie kommen alle in Unit 15 vor.

dinner

swimming

small

managing

casual

evening

_____

_____

_____

_____

_____

_____

talk

costume

dress

dance

clothes

director

B Ordnen Sie die Satzhälften richtig zu.

1. If I could dance,
2. If I were invited to a dinner dance,
3. If it was my fortieth birthday,
4. If I went to a beach party,
5. If I had a computer,
6. If I had to go out with English-speaking customers,

☐ I would invite my friends and family to a party.

☐ I would bring my swimming costume.

[1] I'd go to the dinner dance with you.

☐ I would practise some small talk before I went.

☐ I wouldn't eat anything before I went.

☐ I would work from home a lot.

Can - Could
Von allen Modalverben hat *can* als einziges eine Vergangenheitsform, nämlich *could*.

Bedingungssätze mit *would*

- In Unit 11 haben Sie Bedingungssätze mit *will* gebildet, z.B.
  If it's sunny, I'll go hiking.
  Diese Form wird benutzt, wenn man etwas für wahrscheinlich hält.

- Bei unwahrscheinlichen bzw. hypotetischen Aussagen wird *will* durch
  would ersetzt, und das Zeitwort im *if*-Satz wird vom Present Simple ins
  Past Simple umgewandelt:
  *If it **was** sunny, I **would go** hiking.*

Bedingungssätze
Ein Bedingungssatz kann auch umgedreht werden, so dass zuerst die Folge und anschließend
die Bedingung steht. In diesem Fall steht nach
dem ersten Satzteil **kein** Komma.

C **Bilden Sie Bedingungssätze mit *would*.**

1. I go to South Africa •
   I go to the national parks

   _____

   _____.

2. I am a millionaire • I travel around the world

   _____.

3. I have an evening dress • I wear it to the party

   _____.

4. I have a problem with my computer • I call you

   _____.

5. I can ski • I go skiing with you

   _____.

6. the weather is fine • I go to the beach with you

   _____.

D   Setzen Sie *who* oder *which* in die Relativsätze ein.

1. Do you know someone _____ is good at small talk?

2. Think of a small talk topic _____ is acceptable at an office party.

3. Most companies want people _____ can speak English.

4. Calvados is a traditional apple brandy _____ is made in Normandy.

5. Daniel Radcliffe is the actor _____ plays "Harry Potter".

6. Parma is a town in Italy _____ is famous for its cheese and ham.

> **Who oder which?**
> Als rückbezügliches Fürwort wird **who** bei Personen verwendet, **which** bei Sachen.
> - *My colleagues, **who** can talk easily, always enjoy themselves.*
> - *These are a few ideas **which** will hopefully help you.*

E   Hier sind eine Einladung und ein Dankesschreiben durcheinander geraten. Markieren Sie 'I' für *Invitation* und 'T' für *Thank-you letter*.

Friday, 15th August from 5pm in our garden.

kind invitation. It was a wonderful

Dear neighbours,

Bring a bottle.

of me. I hope we shall see each

delicious. I met a lot of interesting

See you there! Julie and Martin

meet new and old neighbours on

Thank you for your

Let's party! Come along and

other again soon.

Best regards, Paul

Garden Party

people. It was very kind of you to think

Dear Julie and Martin,

party. The food was

F Setzen Sie nun die Teile aus D zu einer Einladung und einem Dankesschreiben zusammen.

Invitation:

Garden Party _____

Dear neighbours, _____

_____

_____

_____

_____

_____

_____

_____

_____

_____

Thank-you letter:

Dear Julie and Martin, _____

_____

_____

_____

_____

_____

_____

_____

_____

_____

_____

_____

_____

G Setzen Sie die Zeitwörter in der richtigen Zeitform ein.

know   think   read   see   like   meet

1. Have you _____ the latest film with Brad Pitt?

2. Did you _____ that this area is famous for its wine?

3. Have you _____ my husband?

4. What do you _____ about our new customer?

5. Do you _____ German food?

6. Have you _____ anything by Agatha Christie?

Unit 16 Revision

A Which town or city is it?

1. Choose a town or a city and describe where it is.
2. The others have to guess the name.

> It's in the USA.
> It's in the south-west by the sea.
> It's a big city, ...

> Is it
> Los Angeles?

> Yes, that's right.

B Find it in the book

1. In groups look through the course book and choose a word, phrase or photo.
2. Tell the other groups your word or phrase, or describe the photo.
3. The other groups have to find it as quickly as possible.

> Dartmouth.

> That's in Unit 13,
> on page 105 in B.

4. The last group to find it has to put the word/phrase into a sentence, or make a sentence about the photo.

C Small talk

1. Sit in a circle and think of a small talk topic, for example the weather or a compliment.
2. Now start a conversation about the topic with the person on your right.
3. Try to keep the conversation going for a while, then talk to the person on your left.

> It's a lovely day, isn't it?

> Yes, hopefully it'll be nice at the weekend, too.

> Oh, do you have plans for the weekend?

> Yes, we're ...

D The other side of the story

1. Listen to one side of a dialogue and read along.
2. Create the other side of the dialogue with a partner.
3. Now roleplay your dialogue.

● Great party, isn't it?

▲ _____

● That's a wonderful costume!

▲ _____

● Where did you find it?

▲ _____

● Really?

▲ _____

● What do you think of that man's costume?

▲ _____

● Kangaroo costumes aren't very good for fancy dress parties, are they?

▲ _____

E Create a crossword puzzle

1. Do this crossword puzzle with a partner.
   All the words are from Unit 13/4.

Across →
1. Artists created it.
2. Not old.
3. You can fly from here.

Down ↓
1. A city in North East England.
2. People walk or cycle on them.
3. The Tyne is a _____.
4. A means of transport.
5. It's bigger than a town.

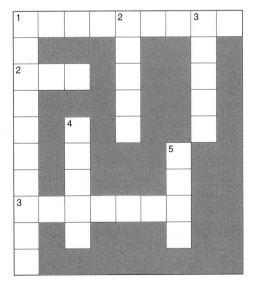

2. Make your own crossword puzzle. Choose a few words from one of the texts or an exercise in the course book. Write descriptions for the words. Then give your crossword to another group to complete.

Grammar Overview

Grammatikübersicht

Ein Pfeil ➜ verweist auf das Kapitel, in dem die jeweilige grammatische Struktur vorkommt bzw. behandelt wird.

Contents Inhalt

Present tenses Gegenwartsformen

to be **Present Simple** *sein* Present Simple		→ Unit 1
Affirmative Bejaht	**Negative** Verneint	**Question** Frageform
I'm (am)	I'm not	Am I?
he/she/it's (is)	he/she/it isn't	Is he/she/it?
we/you/they're (are)	we/you/they aren't	Are we/you/they?

Present Simple: Regular verbs Present Simple: Regelmäßige Verben		→ Unit 1, 3
Affirmative Bejaht	**Negative** Verneint	**Question** Frage
I/you/we/they **need**	I/you/we/they **don't need**	**Do** I/you/we/they **need**?
he/she/it **needs**	he/she/it **doesn't need**	**Does** he/she/it **need**?

Die dritte Person der *Present Simple*-Form wird normalerweise folgendermaßen gebildet:
Grundform des Zeitwortes + **-s**, z. B. *he/she/it needs.*
- Besonderheiten: *go – goes; miss – misses, reach – reaches, wash – washes.*
- Bei Fragen entfällt das **-s** beim Zeitwort; stattdessen wird **-es** an das Hilfszeitwort **do**
  angehängt (*She needs. – Does she need?*)

Present Continuous Verlaufsform		→ Unit 3
Affirmative Bejaht	**Negative** Verneint	**Question** Frage
I'm (am) **working**	I'm not **working**	Am I **working**?
you/we/they're (are) **working**	you/we/they aren't (are not) **working**	Are you/we/they **working**?
he/she/it's (is) **working**	he/she/it isn't (is not) **working**	Is he/she/it **working**?

- Die *Present Continuous*-Form wird folgendermaßen gebildet: **Grundform** des Zeitwortes
  + **-ing**, z. B. *work – working*. Sie bleibt bei allen Personen unverändert.
- Besonderheiten: Das **-e** am Ende eines Zeitworts fällt weg (*make – making*). Bei manchen
  Zeitwörtern, die auf einen **Mitlaut** enden, wird dieser verdoppelt (*sit – sitting, travel –
  travelling*).

Present Continuous vs. Present Simple	→ Unit 3
Present Simple	**Present Continuous**
She's a chef in a restaurant.	At the moment she's **learning** Spanish.

Die *Present Continuous*-Form drückt aus, dass eine Handlung **gerade stattfindet**, im
Gegensatz zur *Present Simple*-Form, die den **Normal-** bzw. **Dauerzustand** beschreibt. (*Present
Continuous* als Zukunftsform siehe Seite 140)

Past tenses Vergangenheitsformen

to be Past Simple *sein* Past Simple		→ Unit 5
Affirmative Bejaht	**Negative** Verneint	**Question** Frage
I/he/she/it **was** you/we/they **were**	I/he/she/it **wasn't** you/we/they **weren't**	**Was** I/he/she/it? **Were** you/we/they?

Regular verbs: Past Simple Regelmäßige Zeitwörter: Past Simple		→ Unit 5
Affirmative Bejaht	**Negative** Verneint	**Question** Frage
She **moved** to Canada.	She **didn't move** to Canada.	**Did** she **move** to Canada?

• Das *Past Simple* drückt eine **abgeschlossene Handlung** in der Vergangenheit aus. Daher ist diese Zeitform häufig in Verbindung mit Zeitangaben wie *last year, three years ago, yesterday* usw. anzutreffen.

• Die *Past Simple*-Form der regelmäßigen Zeitwörter wird durch das Anhängen von -**ed** bzw. -**d** an die Grundform gebildet, z.B. work**ed**, liv**ed**. Sie bleibt bei allen Personen unverändert. Besonderheiten: *travel – travelled, copy – copied*.
Eine Liste der gebräuchlichsten unregelmäßigen Zeitwörter finden Sie auf Seite 146.

Past Continuous vs. Past Simple	→ Unit 6
I **was having** lunch with a friend when her phone suddenly **rang**. A client **called** while I **was driving** home.	

• Das *Past Continuous* ist die Vergangenheitsform vom *Present Continuous: I'm having* lunch *at the moment.* → *I was having* lunch *at this time yesterday.*

• Spricht man von zwei gleichzeitigen Handlungen in der Vergangenheit, so wird das *Past Continuous* für die längere und das *Past Simple* für die kürzere Handlung benutzt.

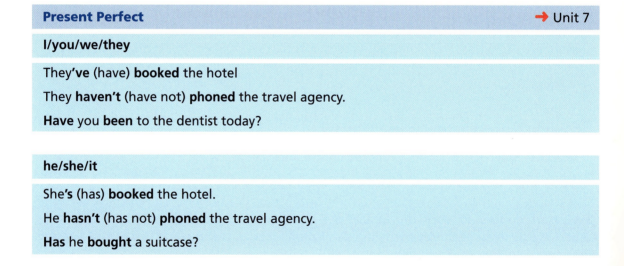

Present Perfect	→ Unit 7
I/you/we/they	
They**'ve** (have) **booked** the hotel They **haven't** (have not) **phoned** the travel agency. **Have** you **been** to the dentist today?	
he/she/it	
She**'s** (has) **booked** the hotel. He **hasn't** (has not) **phoned** the travel agency. **Has** he **bought** a suitcase?	

Das Present Perfect wird mit dem Verb **have** und dem Partizip Perfekt gebildet, z.B. *He has booked*; *They have booked*. Bei regelmäßigen Verben sind Vergangenheitsform und Partizip Perfekt gleich. Eine Liste der unregelmäßigen Verben finden Sie auf Seite 146.

Present Perfect vs. Past Simple	→ Unit 13

They**'ve finished** the new metro line.

The Queen **opened** it as part of her Golden Jubilee Tour.

Yesterday I **walked** along the river.

They**'ve built** new paths for walkers and cyclists along the river.

• Das *Present Perfect* wird häufig benutzt, um über eine Handlung in der Vergangenheit zu sprechen, deren genauer Zeitpunkt nicht wichtig ist: *They'**ve finished** the new metro line.* Hier ist das Ergebnis das Wesentliche, und nicht wann oder wie es dazu gekommen ist.

• Weitere Einzelheiten zum Ereignis – wie z.B. Zeitangaben – werden normalerweise im *Past Simple* genannt: *The Queen **opened** it as part of her Golden Jubilee Tour.*

Passive Passiv

Present Simple Passive	→ Units 10, 14

Service **is included**.

Only top quality materials **are used**.

• Wie im Deutschen haben die Verben im Englischen Aktiv- und Passivformen:
(Aktiv) *They **use** top quality materials.* → (Passiv) *Top quality materials **are used**.*

• Das Passiv wird mit dem Verb *be* und dem Partizip Perfekt gebildet. Bei regelmäßigen Verben sind Vergangenheitsform und Partizip Perfekt gleich. Eine Liste der unregelmäßigen Verben finden Sie auf Seite 146.

Future Zukunft

will	→ Units 10, 11

I**'ll** (will) **have** the smoked salmon.

I**'ll** (will) **go** and **check**.

Monday **will be** sunny and warm.

• *Will* wird hauptsächlich verwendet, wenn man etwas vorhersagt, verspricht, entscheidet oder bestellt.
• *Will* bleibt bei allen Personen unverändert. Die Verneinungsform von *will* ist *will not (won't).*

In the evening we**'re** (are) **going** to the opera.

Das *Present Continuous* wird als Zukunftsform benutzt, wenn es sich um feste Pläne für die absehbare Zukunft handelt.

Modal verbs Modalverben

can

When you speak English you **can** go everywhere.

I **can't** make Friday.

Can you ask her to call me back?

would

I**'d** (would) **wear** casual clothes.

I **wouldn't eat** anything.

Would you like to leave a message.

could

We **could** fit you in this evening.

should

I think people **should** turn off their phones in public places.

If you have flu, you **should** stay in bed.

shall

Shall we go to a café?

might

I **might** leave the house one day.

- Modalverben bleiben bei allen Personen unverändert.
- Verneinungsformen: *can't* (= cannot), *wouldn't, couldn't, shouldn't, shall not, might not.*
- Nur *can* hat eine Vergangenheitsform: *could*

Conditional sentences Bedingungssätze → Unit 11

Conditional with *will* Bedingungsform mit *will*

If it**'s** sunny, I**'ll** (will) **go** hiking.

If it **rains**, I **won't** (will not) **play** tennis.

Spricht man von einer **möglichen** Folge, wird der Bedingungssatz mit *will* gebildet.
• Bedingung: *If* + Verb im *Present Simple: If it's sunny,*
• Folge: *will* + Grundform des Verbs: *I'll go hiking.*

Will bleibt bei allen Personen unverändert. Die Verneinungsform von *will* ist *will not (won't).*

Conditional with *would* Bedingungsform mit *would* → Unit 15

If I **were** you, I**'d** (would) **wear** casual clothes.

Ist die Rede von hypothetischen Aussagen (Annahmen), wird der Bedingungssatz mit *would* gebildet.
• Bedingung: *If* + Verb im *Past Simple: If I were you,*
• Folge: *would* + Grundform des Verbs: *I'd wear casual clothes.*

Ein Bedingungssatz mit *would* kann verwendet werden, um **Ratschläge** zu geben.

Pronouns Fürwörter

Personal pronouns Persönliche Fürwörter → Unit 1, 14

Subject pronoun als Satzgegenstand	Object pronoun als Satzergänzung	Possessive pronoun Besitzanzeigendes Fürwort	
I (ich)	me (mich, mir)	my (mein, meine)	mine (meins)
you	you	your	yours
he	him	his	his
she	her	her	hers
it	it	its	its
we	us	our	ours
you	you	your	yours
they	them	their	theirs

Reflexive Pronouns Rückbezügliche Fürwörter

(I) myself	(he) himself	(it) itself	(you) yourselves
(you) yourself	(she) herself	(we) ourselves	(they) themselves

Beziehen sich Subjekt und Objekt eines Satzes auf eine Person, wird für das Objekt ein rückbezügliches Fürwort verwendet, z.B. *My colleagues always enjoy **themselves**; I have to limit **myself**.*

Indefinite Pronouns Unbestimmte Fürwörter → Unit 14

some / any

Do you have **any** black gloves?

I'm sorry, we don't have **any** in black.

We have **some** in blue.

Relative Pronouns Bezügliche Fürwörter

who / which

All companies want people **who** can speak English.

These are just a few ideas **which** will hopefully help you.

Who wird bei Personen verwendet, *which* bei Sachen.

Articles Geschlechtswörter

Indefinite Article Unbestimmter Artikel	Definite Article Bestimmter Artikel → Unit 3
a restaurant	**the** weather
an office	**the** British

Nouns Hauptwörter

Regular Plural Forms

customer – customer**s**	company – compan**ies**
address – address**es**	tomat**o** – tomat**oes**

Plurals: Exceptions

child – **children**

man – **men**

woman – **women**

foot – **feet**

Genitive 's Genitiv mit 's → Unit 14

Cleopatra**'s** Needle	Harrod**'s**
St. James**'s** Palace	Madame Tussaud**'s**
St. Paul**'s** Cathedral	

Steht das Hauptwort in der Mehrzahl, setzt man das Apostroph hinter das Mehrzahl -s: *Speakers' Corner.*

Adjectives Eigenschaftswörter

Comparison: *-er/-est* Steigerung mit *-er/-est*		→ Unit 2
warm	warm**er**	the warm**est**
sunny	sunn**ier**	the sunn**iest**

Die Komparativ- bzw. Superlativformen von **einsilbigen** Eigenschaftswörtern werden durch das Anhängen von **-er** bzw. **-est** gebildet. Ausnahmen: *good – better – best, bad – worse – worst.*
Bei manchen Eigenschaftswörtern, die auf einen Mitlaut enden, wird dieser verdoppelt: hot – ho**tt**er – ho**tt**est.

Comparison: *more than/the most* Steigerung mit *more than/the most*		→ Unit 2
famous	**more** famous **than**	**the most** famous
popular	**more** popular **than**	**the most** popular

Eigenschaftswörter mit **drei oder mehr Silben** bilden ihre Komparativ- bzw. Superlativform mit **more ... than** und **the most**. Dasselbe gilt für **zweisilbige** Eigenschaftswörter, die nicht auf **-y** enden.

Adverbs/Adverbial phrases Umstandswörter/Umstandsbestimmungen

Formation of Adverbs Bildung der Adverbien		→ Unit 5
slow – slow**ly**	punctual – punctual**ly**	busy – bus**ily**

Adverbien (Umstandswörter) werden in der Regel durch das Anhängen von **-ly** an das Adjektiv (Eigenschaftswort) gebildet.
Ausnahme: *good – **well**, late – **late***

Frequency Häufigkeitsangaben	→ Unit 3, 11
I **always/usually/often/sometimes/never** have breakfast at home.	
I go to the gym **once/twice/three times** a week.	

Häufigkeitsangaben, die aus einem Wort bestehen, werden in der Regel **vor das Zeitwort** gesetzt. Ansonsten stehen Sie **am Ende** des Satzes.

Place Ortsangaben	→ Unit 13
I live **in a small village**.	

Ortsangaben stehen meist am Ende des Satzes.

I moved **to Canada in 1987**.

Zeitangaben stehen in der Regel am Ende des Satzes.
Kommen in einem Satz Orts- **und** Zeitangaben vor, so gilt die Regel „Ort vor Zeit".

Conjunctions Bindewörter

Don't drink **and** drive.

I like Italy **because** the beaches are excellent.

She's a chef in a restaurant, **but** at the moment she's learning Spanish.

You can hike, cycle, play golf **or** go rafting.

The days are longer, **so** you have more time.

Quantifiers Mengenangaben

How much/many → Unit 9

How many people are travelling?

How much (money) is it?

Many wird mit Wörtern verwendet, die „zählbar" sind, d.h. vor die man eine Zahl stellen kann, z. B. *weeks, kilometres.*
Much verwendet man mit „nicht zählbaren" Wörtern, z.B. *water, petrol.*

a few / a little / a lot → Unit 3

a few	fewer	the fewest
a little	less	the least
a lot (of)	more	the most

A few wird mit „zählbaren", *a little* mit „nicht zählbaren" Hauptwörtern verwendet. Besonderheiten: In der gesprochenen Sprache werden *fewer* und *the fewest* zunehmend durch *less* und *the least* ersetzt. *A lot (of)* kann mit „zählbaren" **und** „unzählbaren" Begriffen verwendet werden.

Reported speech Indirekte Rede → Unit 7

"We love driving." They **said** they **loved** driving.

Will man etwas berichten, was in der Vergangenheit gesagt wurde, fängt man den Satz mit einem Zeitwort im *Past Simple* an, z.B. *They said.* Das Hauptverb des Satzes wird dabei ebenfalls ins *Past Simple* gesetzt: *They **said** they **loved** driving.*

The *-ing* form Die *-ing*-Form

-ing after prepositions -ing nach Verhältniswörtern	➜ Unit 3

I look forward to **seeing** you.

Steht ein Verb (Zeitwort) direkt nach einer Präposition (Verhältniswort), so wird *-ing* an das Verb gehängt.

Tag Questions Frageanhängsel ➜ Unit 10, 15

You don't have any Villa Maria wine, **do you**?

It's a beautiful day today, **isn't it**?

- Bei einem verneinten Zeitwort *(don't have)* steht das Frageanhängsel in der bejahten Form: *do you?*
- Nach einem bejahten Zeitwort im Satz *(It's)* steht das Frageanhängsel in der verneinten Form: *isn't it?*

Imperative Befehlsform ➜ Unit 9

Wear a seat belt.   **Don't drink** and **drive**.

In Befehlssätzen wird die **Grundform** des Zeitwortes benutzt. Verneinte Aufforderungen werden mit *don't (do not)* und der Grundform des Zeitwortes gebildet.

Einige nützliche Begriffe

adjective	Eigenschaftswort	**passive**	Passiv
adverb	Umstandswort	**past**	Vergangenheit
affirmative	bejaht	**perfect**	Perfekt
article	Geschlechtswort	**plural**	Mehrzahl
auxiliary	Hilfsverb	**preposition**	Verhältniswort
clause		**present**	Gegenwart
- main ~	Hauptsatz	**pronoun**	Fürwort
- subordinate ~	Nebensatz	**quantifier**	Mengenangabe
conditional	Bedingungsform	**question**	Frage
conjunction	Bindewort	**regular**	regelmäßig
consonant	Mitlaut	**sentence**	Satz
future	Zukunft	**short form**	Kurzform
imperative	Befehlsform	**singular**	Einzahl
infinitive	Grundform	**statement**	Aussage
irregular	unregelmäßig	**subject**	Satzgegenstand
negative	verneint	**tense**	Zeit(form)
noun	Hauptwort	**verb**	Zeitwort *(Wortart)*
object	Satzergänzung	**verb**	Zeitwort *(Satzteil)*
participle	Partizip	**vowel**	Selbstlaut

Unregelmäßige Zeitwörter

Diese Liste enthält die gebräuchlichsten unregelmäßigen Zeitwörter, die im *On the MOVE Refresher Course* vorkommen.

Infinitive Grundform	Past Simple Vergangenheitsform	Past Participle Partizip Perfekt	
be	was, were	been	sein
become	became	become	werden
break	broke	broken	brechen
bring	brought	brought	bringen, mitbringen
build	built	built	bauen
buy	bought	bought	kaufen
choose	chose	chosen	wählen, auswählen
come	came	come	kommen
do	did	done	tun, machen
draw	drew	drawn	zeichnen, malen
drink	drank	drunk	trinken
drive	drove	driven	(Auto) fahren
eat	ate	eaten	essen
feel	felt	felt	fühlen
find	found	found	finden, suchen
fit in	fit in	fit in	einschieben
fly	flew	flown	fliegen
forget	forgot	forgotten	vergessen
get	got	got	bekommen
give	gave	given	geben
go	went	gone	gehen, fahren
grow	grew	grown	wachsen, anbauen
have	had	had	haben
hear	heard	heard	hören
hold	held	held	halten
know	knew	known	kennen, wissen
leave	left	left	verlassen, abfahren
make	made	made	machen
meet	met	met	kennen lernen, treffen
pay	paid	paid	(be)zahlen

put	put	put	legen, stellen
read	read [red]	read [red]	lesen
ride	rode	ridden	reiten, Rad fahren
ring	rang	rung	anrufen, klingeln
run	ran	run	laufen
say	said	said	sagen
see	saw	seen	sehen
sell	sold	sold	verkaufen
send	sent	sent	senden, schicken
sing	sang	sung	singen
sit	sat	sat	sitzen
speak	spoke	spoken	sprechen, reden
spend	spent	spent	ausgeben, verbringen
stand	stood	stood	stehen
steal	stole	stolen	stehlen
swim	swam	swum	schwimmen
take	took	taken	nehmen, mitnehmen
tell	told	told	erzählen, sagen
think	thought	thought	denken
wear	wore	worn	(Kleidung) tragen
write	wrote	written	schreiben

Keys to Practice Section

Übungsteil: Lösungen

Unit 1 *Getting to know each other*

A
1. my   3. His   5. their
2. Her   4. our   6. your

B

-s	-ies	irregular
hotels	countries	grand-
customers	dictionaries	children
groups	companies	women
names		men

C Her name's Maria Lopez. She's from Barcelona in Spain. She loves sport and travelling abroad. She works for a travel agency and needs English for her job.

D
1. Hi! How are you?
2. Not so bad, thanks. And you?
3. I'm fine, thanks. By the way, this is Chris.
4. Hello, Chris. Nice to meet you.
5. Nice to meet you, too.
6. Well, have a nice evening.
7. Thanks. You too. Goodbye.
8. Bye!

E
1. He often shows customers around their production department.
2. She travels a lot in her job.
3. Their grandchildren speak English.
4. He's unemployed at the moment.
5. They travel abroad a lot.

F
1. I'm from Paris.
2. How are you?
3. He's unemployed at the moment.
4. Sometimes there are customers from other countries.
5. This is our production department.
6. There's one travel agency.

G

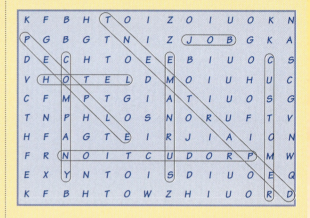

Unit 2 *People and countries*

A
1. excellent   – drei- oder mehrsilbig
2. great   – einsilbig
3. friendly   – zweisilbig
4. popular   – drei- oder mehrsilbig
5. cheap   – einsilbig
6. bad   – einsilbig
7. comfortable – drei- oder mehrsilbig
8. clean   – einsilbig

B friendly – expensive – cheaper – bad – famous – sunnier – beautiful – best

C
1. beach
2. restaurant
3. summer
4. accommodation
5. people
6. moment
Lösungswort: Europe

D
1. I'd like to speak to Samantha Brown, please.
2. I'm afraid Samantha isn't in at the moment.
3. Yes, of course.
4. My name's Freud, Annabel Freud.

E
1. What's your name, please?
2. How do you spell that?
3. Can you ask him to call me back?
4. What's your telephone number?
5. Would you like to leave a message?
6. Can I leave a message?

F

-ish	-ese	-an
Swedish	Japanese	Italian
Finnish	Portuguese	German
Polish		Russian
Spanish		Austrian
Danish		Norwegian

Unit 3 *Working in Europe*

A
1. He's playing the piano.
2. They're playing tennis.
3. He's reading a/the newspaper.
4. He's looking after the children. / He's making sandwiches for the children.
5. She's drinking coffee.

B
1. She's an engineer.
2. He's a chef.
3. She works in an office.
4. They work on a farm.
5. He works in a restaurant.
6. There's an internet café.

C
people
boring, famous, unfriendly, terrible, helpful, friendly, interesting, unhelpful, popular
weather
hot, terrible, rainy, cold, sunny

D
1. Paul always reads the newspaper.
2. Anne sometimes looks after the children.
3. Paul usually goes shopping at the weekend.
4. Anne never makes breakfast.
5. Paul sometimes drinks coffee.
6. Anne often goes cycling.

E
is – lives – likes – doesn't speak – isn't working – 's doing – 's learning – meets – go

F
1. Do you read a daily newspaper?
2. Do you have breakfast at home?
3. Does he enjoy his job?
4. Does she use French in her job?
5. Do they have an easy job?
6. Do you go on holiday in winter?

G
1. a few
2. less
3. fewer
4. Fewer

Unit 5 *Looking back*

A
1. Yes, **I did.**
2. No, **I didn't.**
3. Yes, **I did.**
4. Yes, **I was.**
5. No, **I didn't.**
6. No, **I didn't.**
7. Oh, yes, **I was.**

B
was – started – left – was – was – went – was – moved – met – worked – bought – renovated – opened

C
1. Did you go to school in England?
2. Did you like school?
3. Did you enjoy travelling when you were young?
4. Were you happy in England?
5. Did you work for a travel company in Chicago?
6. Was your job interesting?
7. Did you meet your partner in Chicago?
8. Did you have your own flat?

D
1. Good morning.
2. Fine, thanks.
3. Thanks.
4. Yes, please.
5. Nice to meet you, Ms Goodall.

E
1. great, efficiently
2. badly, terrible
3. punctually, productive
4. punctual, late, slow
5. independent
6. good, well

Unit 6 *Then and now*

A was – lived – went – came – worked – grew – had – was – didn't have – finished – left – went – didn't find – met – started

B
1. How long did you live in Canada?
2. What did you do in Canada?
3. How did you find a job?
4. Where did you live?
5. When did you come back to Europe?

C
1. **What did you do** after school?
2. **When did you** start work there?
3. **How long did you work** there?
4. **What did you do?**
5. **When did you move back** to England?
6. **How old** are you?

D
1. was having, called
2. was reading, came
3. met, was walking
4. was writing, rang
5. started, was talking
6. was having, arrived
7. was waiting, asked

E
1. friends   5. sport
2. theatre   6. holiday
3. tennis   7. camping
4. travel   8. cinema
Lösungswort: free time

F **Regular**
enjoy, move, learn, start, finish, travel, walk, talk, call
Irregular
do, go, buy, meet, be, write, have, make, get, read, find

Unit 7 *Holidays*

A
1. gone   5. grown
2. done   6. been
3. left   7. had
4. got   8. come

B
1. Tom has **collected the tickets.**
2. They've both **phoned their parents.**
3. They haven't **bought food for the journey.**
4. They've both **cancelled the newspaper.**
5. Anita **has packed her suitcase.**
6. Tom **hasn't packed his suitcase.**
7. Anita **hasn't organized the taxi to the station.**

C
1. half past one, one thirty
2. eight o'clock
3. quarter past twelve, twelve fifteen
4. quarter to four, three forty-five
5. three o'clock
6. quarter to ten, nine forty-five
7. half past eleven, eleven thirty

D
1. read   4. found
2. cancelled   5. made
3. written   6. phoned

E
● I'd like to **make** an appointment, please.
▲ Yes, certainly. **Let** me check. What about Thursday 4th?
● Oh, I'm **afraid** I can't make Thursday.
▲ Well, we could **fit** you **in** tomorrow morning.
● Yes, that's fine. **What** time?
▲ **Would** nine thirty be convenient?
● Yes, that's **great.**

F
1. They said this was their first trip to England.
2. They said they liked the food.
3. They said their hotel was very good.
4. They said they didn't like driving in England.
5. They said they were having a great time.
6. They said they were looking forward to going to London at the end of their trip.

Unit 9 *A trip down under*

A
1. Next week we**'re going** to Verona to the opera, and the next day we**'re sightseeing**.
2. Sorry, I can't come to your party on Saturday because I**'m visiting** my parents.
3. What **are** you **doing** on Thursday evening? We**'re having** a little party here. Can you come?
4. On Saturday I**'m playing** tennis in the afternoon, but I can come and see you in the evening.
5. We**'re driving** to London in the morning, and **going** shopping. But we can meet in the evening.
6. They've cancelled my flight, so I**'m taking** the train instead.

B
On Monday I'm **playing golf with Barbara**.
On Tuesday I**'m visiting George in hospital**.
On Wednesday I**'m collecting the tickets from the travel agency**.
On Thursday I**'m going to the opera with Daniel**.
On Friday I**'m packing my suitcase**.
At the weekend I**'m going to Berlin**.

C
1. much
2. many
3. much
4. many
5. much
6. many
7. much

D
1. Book
2. Check
3. Don't forget
4. Make
5. Don't be late
6. Call

E
1. microwave
2. cheese
3. flight
4. colour TV
5. bicycle
6. office

F
▲ Royal Hotel, good morning, **can** I help you?
■ Good morning. I**'d like** to book a room, please.
▲ Yes, certainly. Double or single?
■ A double room, please.
▲ And **when** is it for?
■ 15th of June.
▲ **How many** nights, please?
■ Five nights. **How much** is it?
▲ $40 per night, so $200 in total.
■ OK. That's fine.
▲ **So that's** one double room for five nights arriving, on June 15th.
■ That's right.
▲ And **what's** the name, please?

Unit 10 *Eating out*

A
1. I'll close the window.
2. I'll have the chicken.
3. We'll have the Chianti.
4. Yes, OK. I'll go.
5. No, but Kate will be there.
6. Don't worry, I'll show you.

B
1. is served
2. are served
3. are served
4. is served
5. is served
6. is included

C
1. You don't have any Australian wine, **do you**?
2. You like Irish music, **don't you**?
3. They hate fish, **don't they**?
4. You don't like Italian food, **do you**?
5. He doesn't speak English, **does he**?
6. She plays tennis very well, **doesn't she**?

D
1. **Shall we go** to a restaurant?
2. **What** would you like to eat?
3. **Do** you like Indian food?
4. **How about** Italian?
5. **When** shall we meet?
6. **Are you** ready to order?
7. **Can I have** the chicken without mushrooms?
8. **Anything** else?

E
▲ What shall we do this evening?
■ Let's go to the cinema!
● I went to the cinema yesterday. Why don't we go out for dinner?
▲ That's a good idea!

- ■ I'd prefer to go to the pub. Restaurants are expensive.
- ● Not always! How about the new Italian restaurant? It's very good value for money.
- ▲ Oh yes! The food there's delicious.
- ■ I don't like pizza.
- ● You can have pasta then!
- ▲ Come on, let's go! I'm hungry.

F

Unit 11 *Health and Body*

A

B
1. When you're stressed you should try yoga.
2. When I have a cold I drink plenty of tea.
3. When I have backache I go swimming.

4. When I have flu I normally stay in bed.
5. When I do sport I feel good.
6. If you think you have broken your arm you should go to hospital.

C
1. **Don't eat** a lot of fruit.
2. **Smoke** a lot.
3. **Drink** plenty of coffee.
4. **Don't do** sport.
5. **Don't go** hiking.
6. **Watch** plenty of television.

D
1. sunny
2. rain
3. sunny periods
4. cloudy
5. sunny and showers
6. thunderstorms

E
it'll be – will be – sunny – will have – showers – periods – there'll be sunshine – cloudy – there'll be rain – thunderstorms

F
1. If you give me your phone number, I**'ll call you next week**.
2. If I have time on Saturday, I**'ll come and see you**.
3. If you eat plenty of fresh fruit and vegetables, you**'ll be healthier**.
4. If it's sunny next weekend, we**'ll go cycling**.
5. If you organize the food, I**'ll buy the drinks**.

G
1. head	5. fingers	9. arm
2. nose	6. leg	10. neck
3. ear	7. foot	11. mouth
4. shoulder	8. knee	12. eye

Unit 13 *Places*

A
1. on – in – of – from
2. by – near – from

B
1. get off	4. get around
2. get to	5. gets on
3. get on	

152

C
1. They've finished the new underground line.
2. They haven't opened a new shopping centre.
3. They haven't built a new indoor swimming pool.
4. They've created a new industrial area outside the town centre.
5. They've renovated a lot of the historical buildings in town.
6. They've opened a few new restaurants.
7. They haven't moved the post office to the station.

D haven't written – have had – said – found – moved – started – has been – I've enclosed

E
1. since   3. since   5. since
2. for   4. for   6. since

F
1. Sie leben seit zwei Jahren hier.
2. Sie hat seit drei Monaten ihre Kreditkarte nicht mehr benutzt.
3. Stephen arbeitet seit fünf Jahren dort.

G sea – river
bus – underground
mountain – hill
city – village
north – east
school – university
coffee shop – restaurant
change – purse

Unit 14 *Shopping*

A
1. any, some   4. any
2. any, any, some   5. Some
3. some   6. any

B
1. **any**thing
2. **Some**body **some**where
3. **some**one
4. **any**thing
5. **some**thing

6. **some**one
7. **any**one
8. **any**thing

C
1. Only top quality materials are used.
2. All our tables are made to the highest standards.
3. These tables are sold all over the world.
4. Your satisfaction is guaranteed.
5. All main dishes are served with a side salad.
6. Most reservations are made online.

D
1. in   4. in   6. to
2. from   5. to   7. by
3. on

E
1. Good morning. Can I help you?
2. I'd like a kilo of apples, please.
3. No, I'm sorry, we don't have any in black.
4. Would you sign here, please?
5. I'm just looking, thanks.

F
1. cash   3. newspaper
2. coat   4. telephone

G
1. I'd like to speak to someone in the customer services department, please.
2. One moment, please, I'll put you through.
3. I'm sorry, the line's busy.
4. Would you like to hold?
5. I'm calling about a reservation I made last week.

Unit 15 *Party Time*

A dinner dance
swimming costume
small talk
managing director
casual clothes
evening dress

B

1. If I could dance, I'd go to the dinner dance with you.
2. If I were invited to a dinner dance, I wouldn't eat anything before I went.
3. If it was my fortieth birthday, I would invite my friends and family to a party.
4. If I went to a beach party, I would bring my swimming costume.
5. If I had a computer, I would work from home a lot.
6. If I had to go out with English-speaking customers, I would practise some small talk before I went.

C

1. If I went to South Africa, I'd go to the national parks.
2. If I were a millionaire, I'd travel around the world.
3. If I had an evening dress, I'd wear it to the party.
4. If I had a problem with my computer, I'd call you.
5. If I could ski, I'd go skiing with you.
6. If the weather was fine, I'd go to the beach with you.

D

1. who	4. which
2. which	5. who
3. who	6. which

E+F

Invitation:
Garden Party
Dear neighbours,
Let's party! Come along and meet new and old neighbours on Friday, 15th August from 5pm in our garden.
Bring a bottle.
See you there!
Julie and Martin

Thank-you letter:
Dear Julie and Martin,
Thank you for your kind invitation. It was a wonderful party. The food was delicious. I met a lot of interesting people. It was very kind of you to think of me.
I hope we shall see each other again soon.
Best regards,
Paul

G

1. seen	4. think
2. know	5. like
3. met	6. read

Tapescripts

Hörtexte

Unit 1 *Getting to know each other*

1B

1. I need English for my job. I often show customers around our production department. Sometimes there are groups from other countries, so I need to explain everything in English.
2. I work for a travel agency. I travel a lot in my job. I often go and look at hotels in Finland and other European countries and English is spoken everywhere.
3. Our daughter-in-law is Canadian, and our grandchildren speak English. They live in Canada. We want to visit them in the summer.
4. I'm unemployed at the moment. English is very important for me because all companies want people who can speak English.
5. We love travelling, and we travel abroad a lot. When you speak English you can go everywhere.

3A

- ■ Hi!
- ▲ Hello!
- ■ How are you?
- ▲ Not so bad, thanks, and how are you?
- ■ I'm fine, thank you.
- ▲ By the way, this is Nicole. She's from Jena. She needs English for her job.
- ■ Hello, Nicole, nice to meet you.
- ● Hello, nice to meet you, too.
- ■ Well, have a nice evening.
- ▲ Thank you. You too.
- ■ See you next week.
- ▲ OK, see you. Bye.
- ● Goodbye.

3B

1. Hi. How are you?
2. Not so bad, thanks.
3. Nice to meet you.
4. Nice to meet you, too.
5. Have a nice evening.
6. Thank you.
7. See you next week.
8. Goodbye.

Unit 2 *People and Countries*

2B

German coffee and cake on Sunday at three, when the British have biscuits with tea. But the French like lunch with wine in tall glasses, and the Irish drink beer by the sea.

Finnish fish is famous in hot and cold dishes, whilst Swedish meatballs are spicy and sweet. But the Danish prefer pastries with custard and sugar, and Austrian pancakes are delicious to eat.

The Spanish wish for sausage with spices, whilst the Dutch do much for cheese. But Italian pizzas are eaten in millions, and Portuguese wine goes down with great ease.

Belgian chocolates and truffles have many admirers, whilst Greek tzatziki is simply a must, and the Luxembourg luxury is cooking fine sauces, so in Europe you can eat till you drop!

3A

- ▲ Hello.
- ■ Hello, I'd like to speak to Helen Brown, please.
- ▲ I'm afraid Helen isn't in at the moment. Would you like to leave a message?
- ■ Yes, please. Can you ask her to call me back? My name's Rivero, Martin Rivero.
- ▲ Yes, of course. How do you spell that, please?
- ■ It's R – I – V – E – R – O.
- ▲ And what's your telephone number?
- ■ It's oh four oh, seven six three, two one, double two.
- ▲ OK. I've got it.
- ■ Great. Thanks a lot.
- ▲ You're welcome. Bye.

3D

1. h - e - l - l - o
2. p - e - o - p - l -e
3. f - r - i - e - n - d - l - y
4. P - o - r - t - u - g - u - e - s - e

Unit 3 *Working in Europe*

2A

1. Do you have breakfast at home?
2. Do you forget names?
3. Do you use English in your job?
4. Do you read a daily newspaper?
5. Do you go shopping at the weekend?
6. Do you enjoy your work?
7. Do you go on holiday in winter?

Unit 5 *Looking Back*

1B

I was born in England, but I moved to Canada with my parents in 1987 when I was 17 years old. At first I missed my friends but I soon started to like my new home. I learned a lot of new sports, like ice-hockey and basketball, but most of all I enjoyed camping in the mountains. I first visited the Rockies when I was 20 years old. In 1991 I finished college and I started work with an airline company. For the next three years I travelled a lot in North and South America, however I always liked the Rockies best. I met my partner in 1995. Last year we bought an old farmhouse and renovated it together. Now I run a small business which organizes camping holidays for teenagers.

1E

1. moved, missed, learned, enjoyed, finished, travelled, liked
2. started, renovated

3A

▲ Good morning Jane.
■ Hello, Patricia.
▲ I have a meeting with Charles, he's expecting me at 10.
■ Oh, I'm afraid he's still in a meeting. Why don't you take a seat? Would you like a cup of coffee?
▲ Yes, please, that would be great. I can look through my reviews while I'm waiting.
■ Good! Milk and sugar?
▲ Milk, but no sugar, please.

3B

Charles: So, Patricia, tell me about your new employee. Do we have the right person for the job?

Patricia: Well yes, I think so. Amanda started

work in the purchasing department six months ago and we are all very impressed. She works very well in the team. She completes all tasks efficiently and uses her time productively. She worked on quite an important project last month and communicated very effectively with the other members of the group. What more can I say? She's always punctual. Perfect really, a great asset for the company.

Unit 6 *Then and now*

2A+B

■ What did you do when you left school?
● When I left school I went to secretarial college for a year, then I found a job at the United Nations in New York and started work in 1967.
■ That sounds interesting. How long did you work there?
● I only worked there for two years. That was long enough!
■ What did you do?
● I worked as a secretary.
■ Did you have your own office?
● No, I shared an office with a colleague. We each had a typewriter and a desk and chair – that was it! Not like today.
■ Did you like your job?
● The work wasn't very interesting, and so when I saw an advert for a job in the UK, I wrote to the company immediately.
■ When did you get your first computer and fax machine?
● I got my first computer in 1986, it made my job much easier. We got a fax machine in 1995, but nowadays I send more e-mails than faxes.
■ How did you copy documents before photocopiers?
● I used a duplicating machine. It wasn't always very easy to use. There was a photo copier in the building somewhere, but they weren't very common in those days and they were very expensive, too.
■ How did you contact people before e-mail?
● If we wanted to contact someone quickly, we used the telephone or telex machine. And if that failed we had to send a letter which of course is much slower – even today.
■ And, do you still work in an office today?
● Today I have an office at home, it's much more practical.

4A

1. <u>v</u>egetables – tele<u>v</u>ision – <u>v</u>ery – con<u>v</u>ersation – expensi<u>v</u>e – <u>v</u>isiting
2. dish<u>w</u>asher – <u>w</u>ork – <u>w</u>hat – <u>w</u>hen – <u>w</u>ith - <u>w</u>alking – <u>w</u>ant

Unit 7 *Holidays*

1C

● Hello.
■ Hi, David, it's me. Have you booked the hotel for our holiday? I can't find the booking confirmation.
● Yes, I've booked the hotel, but I haven't phoned the travel agent about the car rental.
■ Oh, I've already organized the car rental, and I've collected the airline tickets.
● Have you checked the tickets?
■ Yes, I have. They're OK. Have you packed anything?
● No! I need a new suitcase, but I haven't bought one yet.
■ Oh dear. By the way, what are you doing about your newspaper?
● I've cancelled it.
■ That's a good idea.
● So, see you soon.
■ Yes, see you. Bye!
● Bye.

2B

■ Good afternoon, Oakley Dental Surgery.
▲ Hello. I'd like to make an appointment with Dr Kent, please.
■ Certainly. Have you been here before?
▲ Yes. My name's Martha Burns.
■ Oh yes, Mrs Burns. Let me check. What about Friday the 13th at two thirty?
▲ Oh, I'm afraid I can't make Friday the 13th. I'm going on holiday on the 12th and would like a check-up before I go.
■ Well, we could fit you in this evening.
▲ Yes, that's fine. What time?
■ Would five thirty be convenient?
▲ Yes, that's OK. Thanks very much.
■ You're welcome. Goodbye.
▲ Bye.

2C

1. Friday the 13th at two thirty
2. Monday the 5th at ten fifteen
3. Thursday the 31st at nine o'clock
4. Wednesday the 12th at six

Unit 9 *A trip down under*

2C

▲ Good morning, Motorhomes and More, how can I help you?
■ Hello, I'd like to make a booking, please.
▲ Certainly, which motorhome would you like?
■ I'd like to book the Regent for two weeks.
▲ OK, when do you want to travel?
■ From the 20th of August until the 3rd of September.
▲ OK, and how many people are travelling?
■ Two adults and three children.
▲ And approximately how many kilometres are you travelling?
■ About 3000.
▲ So that's two weeks, 3000 kilometres, from 20th August until 8th September.
■ Yes, that's right. And how much is that?
▲ That's AUS$1900 all inclusive.

3B

1. motorhome
2. approximately
3. microwave
4. kilometres
5. kangaroo
6. Australia

Unit 10 *Eating out*

4A

▲ Are you ready to order?
■ Yes, I'd like the garlic cheese bread as a starter, and then the seafood Laksa.
▲ I'm sorry, madam, the Laksa is off, but I can recommend the warm smoked salmon, it's very good.
■ Oh, OK I'll take the smoked salmon then, but can I have it with rice instead of the baked potato?
▲ Yes, of course. And you, sir?
■ Well, I'll have the ham and melon mix as a starter, and then I'll have the vegetarian pasta for my main course but without the parmesan, please.
▲ Certainly. And anything else? I can recommend some very good local wines.
■ Oh, you don't have any Villa Maria wine, do you?
▲ I'll just go and check!
■ That would be great.

Unit 11 *Health and Body*

3C

Sit with your back straight.
1. Lift your right leg and point your toes for five seconds, then relax. Repeat with your left leg.
2. Lift your right leg and pull your foot back for five seconds, then relax. Repeat with your left leg.
3. Now stand up with your back straight and pull your shoulder blades together for five seconds, then relax.
4. Raise your arms and stretch as high as you can for five seconds.
Now close your eyes. Take a deep breath. Breathe out slowly and open your eyes.

4C

And here is the weekly weather report. For the start of the week, the weather will be sunny and warm with temperatures in the twenties. Wednesday will be changeable with sunshine and showers, and a little colder in the evening. Thursday will be cloudy and windy, and rain is forecast for Friday, so remember to take an umbrella with you. You can look forward to a good weekend with some hot and sunny periods, ending with thunderstorms on Sunday.

Unit 12 *Revision*

D

Simon says stand up. Simon says raise your right arm. Simon says raise your left leg. Sit down. Simon says sit down. Close your eyes. Simon says raise your left arm. Stretch as high as you can. Simon says point your toes. Relax. Simon says close your eyes. Take a deep breath. Simon says open your eyes. Stand up. Simon says relax. Simon says take a deep breath. Simon says breathe out slowly.

Unit 13 *Places*

2B

▲ London Travel information, can I help you?
● Hello, can you tell me how to get to the Tate Gallery?
▲ Where are you travelling from?
● Heathrow airport.
▲ OK. The easiest way is to get on the underground and take the Piccadilly Line into London. Then you should change to the Circle Line at South Kensington and travel to Westminster. Get off the underground at Westminster and then take the 77A bus, travelling towards Lambeth Bridge. The 77A will stop at the Tate Gallery.
● So that's the Piccadilly Line to South Kensington, the Circle Line to Westminster and then the 77A bus to the Tate Gallery. Great, thank you very much.
▲ You're welcome.

3A

● Excuse me. I've left my umbrella on the underground. Can you help me?
▲ Have you asked in the lost property office?

● Oh no. I don't have any change for the ticket machine.
▲ Don't worry. You can use your debit card instead.

● Hello. Can you help me, please? Someone has stolen my purse.
▲ Oh dear, I am sorry. You should go to the police.

Unit 14 *Shopping*

2B

1. Is that all?
2. How much is it?
3. Do you accept cheques?
4. Could you wrap it, please?
5. Do you have a store card?
6. How would you like to pay?
7. Would you sign here, please?
8. I'm just looking, thanks.

2C

■ Do you have any black gloves?
▲ Just let me check for you. No I'm sorry, we don't have any in black, but we have some in blue.
■ No that's OK, thank you. I'll just take the scarf.
▲ OK. Is that all?
■ Yes. How much is it?
▲ That's 19.99. Do you have a store card?
■ No, I don't.
▲ How would you like to pay?
■ By credit card, please.
▲ Would you sign here, please? ... Here's your receipt. Thank you very much.
■ Thank you. Goodbye.
▲ Bye.

3B

■ Good morning, Home Comforts, can I help you?
▲ Good morning, I'd like to speak to someone in the customer services department, please.
■ One moment please, I'll put you through.
▲ Good morning, customer services.
■ Oh hello, I'm calling about a coffee table I ordered from you recently. It was delivered this morning, but the glass top is broken.
▲ Oh, I'm sorry, that is a problem. What's your order number? ...

Unit 15 *Social events*

3C

1. ■ Have you seen the latest Steven Spielberg film?
   ▲ No, I haven't. Is it good?

2. ■ Did you know that this area is famous for its cheese?
   ▲ Oh really? How interesting.

3. ■ Have you met the new managing director yet?
   ▲ No, not yet. What's she like?

4. ■ What a wonderful dress!
   ▲ Thank you very much.

5. ■ What do you think about our latest product?
   ▲ I think it's great.

6. ■ It's a beautiful day today, isn't it?
   ▲ Yes, hopefully it'll be nice at the weekend.

Unit 16 *Revision*

D

● Great party, isn't it?

● That's a wonderful costume!

● Where did you find it?

● Really?

● Kangaroo costumes aren't very good for fancy dress parties, are they?

● And they're always so hot!

Unit Vocabulary
Lektionsbegleitendes-Wörterverzeichnis

Die Wörter sind in chronologischer Reihenfolge unter der jeweiligen Lektions- und Übungsnummer aufgenommen, z.B. 1/1A (Unit 1, Teil 1, Übung A).
Wörter, die mehr als eine Bedeutung haben, werden nochmals an der entsprechenden Stelle aufgeführt.

(AE) = amerikanisches Englisch   *(BE)* = britisches Englisch

Phonetic alphabet Lautschrift

[:] bedeutet, dass der vorangehende Laut lang ist.
['] bedeutet, dass die folgende Silbe die Hauptbetonung erhält.
[ˌ] bedeutet, dass die folgende Silbe eine Nebenbetonung erhält.

[ɪ]	is	[i:]	meet	[eɪ]	name	[p]	piano	[ʃ]	shop
[e]	hello	[ɑ:]	park	[aɪ]	my	[b]	bus	[ʒ]	usually
[æ]	at	[ɔ:]	for	[ɔɪ]	appointment	[t]	to	[h]	hotel
[ʌ]	number	[u:]	afternoon	[əʊ]	no	[d]	need	[tʃ]	children
[ɒ]	office	[ɜ:]	purse	[aʊ]	town	[k]	speak	[dʒ]	just
[ʊ]	good			[ɪə]	here	[g]	good	[m]	morning
[ə]	number	[ɔ̃:]	restaurant	[eə]	where	[f]	first	[n]	nice
				[ʊə]	you're	[v]	evening	[ŋ]	long
						[θ]	thanks	[l]	left
						[ð]	this	[r]	room
						[s]	seven	[w]	work
						[z]	is	[j]	yes

Unit 1 *Getting to know each other*

1

to get to know someone — jemanden kennen lernen
[tʊ getˌtʊ 'nəʊ ˌsʌmwʌn]
each other [ˌi:tʃ 'ʌðə] — einander
to need [tʊ ni:d] — brauchen

1/1A

under ['ʌndə] — unter
I work for a travel agency — ich arbeite bei einem Reisebüro
[aɪ ˌwɜːk fərˌə 'trævl̩ˌeɪdʒənsɪ]
daughter-in-law — Schwiegertochter
['dɔːtərɪnlɔː]
travelling ['trævəlɪŋ] — Reisen
often ['ɒftn] ['ɒfn] — oft, häufig
to show customers around — Kunden herumführen
[tʊ ʃəʊ 'kʌstəməzˌəˌraʊnd]
production department — Produktionsabteilung
[prə'dʌkʃn dɪˌpɑːtmənt]

I'm unemployed at the moment [aɪm ˌʌnɪm'plɔɪd ətˌðə ˌməʊmənt] — ich bin zur Zeit arbeitslos

1/1B

to complete [tʊ kəm'pli:t] — vervollständigen
important [ɪm'pɔːtənt] — wichtig
sometimes ['sʌmtaɪmz] — manchmal
other countries — andere Länder
[ˌʌðə 'kʌntrɪz]
to explain everything — alles erklären
[tʊ ɪk'spleɪn ˌevrɪθɪŋ]
to look at [tʊ 'lʊk æt] — anschauen, besichtigen
English is spoken everywhere — Englisch wird überall gesprochen
[ˌɪŋglɪʃ ɪzˌspəʊkn 'evrɪweə]
our grandchildren — unsere Enkelkinder
[aʊə 'grænˌtʃɪldrən]
company ['kʌmpənɪ] — Firma
to travel abroad — ins Ausland reisen
[tʊ ˌtrævl ə'brɔːd]

1/1C

form [fɔːm]	Formular
first name ['fɜːst ˌneɪm]	Vorname
surname ['sɜːneɪm]	Nach-, Familienname
reason ['riːzn]	Grund

1/1D

introduce yourself [ˌɪntrəˈdjuːs jɔːˌself]	stellen Sie sich vor
nice to meet you [ˌnaɪs tʊ ˈmiːt ˌjuː]	nett, Sie kennenzu-lernen

1/2

word collection ['wɜːd kəˌlekʃn]	Wörtersammlung

1/2A

to label [tʊ ˈleɪbl]	beschriften
pen [pen]	Stift
dictionary ['dɪkʃənrɪ]	Wörterbuch
mobile phone [ˌməʊbaɪl ˈfəʊn]	Mobiltelefon, Handy

1/2B

to collect [tʊ kəˈlekt]	sammeln
how many [haʊ ˈmenɪ]	wie viele

1/Text

English-speaking countries [ˌɪŋglɪʃˌspiːkɪŋ ˈkʌntrɪz]	englischsprachige Länder
only ['əʊnlɪ]	nur
neutral ['njuːtrl]	neutral
is used more and more often [ɪz juːzd ˌmɔːrˌən mɔːrˌˈɒftn]	wird immer häufiger benutzt
married ['mærɪd]	verheiratet

1/3A

How are you? [ˌhaʊ ə ˈjuː]	Wie geht es Ihnen/dir?
not so bad [ˌnɒt səʊ ˈbæd]	nicht schlecht
I'm fine. [aɪm ˈfaɪn]	Mir geht es gut.
by the way [ˌbaɪ ðə ˈweɪ]	übrigens
Have a nice evening. [ˌhæv ə naɪs ˈiːvnɪŋ]	Ich wünsche Ihnen einen schönen Abend.
See you next week. [ˌsiː jʊ nekst ˈwiːk]	Bis nächste Woche.
see you ['siː ˌjuː]	bis dann

1/QQ

to match [tʊ mætʃ]	zuordnen

Unit 2 *People and Countries*

2/1

friendliest ['frendlɪɪst]	freundlichste

2/1A

following a survey [ˌfɒləʊɪŋ ə ˈsɜːveɪ]	laut einer Umfrage
reader ['riːdə]	Leser/in
newspaper ['njuːzˌpeɪpə]	Zeitung
to report [tʊ rɪˈpɔːt]	berichten
popular ['pɒpjələ]	beliebt
holiday destination [ˌhɒlɪdeɪ ˌdestɪˈneɪʃn]	Urlaubsziel
an official [ən əˈfɪʃl]	(hier) Sprecher
National Tourist Board [ˌnæʃnl ˈtʊərɪst ˌbɔːd]	Nationaler Tourismusverband
first of all ['fɜːst əv ˌɔːl]	zuerst
not just famous for [ˌnɒt ˈdʒʌst feɪməs fɔː]	nicht nur berühmt für
to hike [tʊ haɪk]	wandern
to cycle [tʊ ˈsaɪkl]	Rad fahren
to play golf [tʊ pleɪ ˈɡɒlf]	Golf spielen
to go rafting [tʊ ɡəʊ ˈrɑːftɪŋ]	zum Rafting gehen
beach [biːtʃ]	Strand
cleaner ['kliːnə]	sauberer
accommodation [əˌkɒməˈdeɪʃn]	Unterkunft
food [fuːd]	Essen
comfortable ['kʌmftəbl]	bequem, komfortabel
a lot of [ə ˈlɒt əv]	viel(e)
different restaurants [ˌdɪfrənt ˈrestərɒ̃ŋz] [ˌdɪfrənt ˈrestərɒnts]	verschiedene Restaurants
cheaper ['tʃiːpə]	billiger

2/1B

syllable ['sɪləbl]	Silbe

2/1C

favourite ['feɪvərɪt]	Lieblings~

2/1D

pairwork ['peəwɜːk]	Partnerarbeit
to give [tʊ ɡɪv]	geben, angeben
because [bɪˈkɒz]	weil
So do I. [ˌsəʊ dʊˈaɪ]	Ich auch.

2/2A

to associate [tʊ əˈsəʊʃɪeɪt]	assoziieren
to spell [tʊ spel]	buchstabieren
on the board [ɒn ðə ˈbɔːd]	an der Tafel

2/2B

listen and tick [ˌlɪsn ən ˈtɪk]	hören Sie zu und kreuzen Sie an

2/3A

to be in [tʊ bɪˈɪn]	zu Hause sein
caller [ˈkɔːlə]	Anrufer/in
I'd like [aɪd ˈlaɪk]	ich möchte
I'm afraid [aɪm əˈfreɪd]	ich fürchte
to call [tʊ kɔːl]	anrufen
again [əˈgen] [əˈgeɪn]	wieder
to leave a message [tʊ liːv ə ˈmesɪdʒ]	eine Nachricht hinterlassen

2/3C

of course [əv ˈkɔːs]	natürlich

2/3D

pronunciation [prəˌnʌnsɪˈeɪʃn]	Aussprache
spelling [ˈspelɪŋ]	Schreibweise
to practise [tʊ ˈpræktɪs]	üben

2/3E

role play [ˈrəʊlpleɪ]	Rollenspiel

2/PS

bed and breakfast places [ˌbed ən ˈbrekfəst ˌpleɪsɪz]	Frühstückspensionen
probably [ˈprɒbəblɪ]	wahrscheinlich
countryside [ˈkʌntrɪsaɪd]	Landschaft
beautiful [ˈbjuːtɪfʊl]	schön

Unit 3 *Working in Europe*

3/1A

in an office [ɪn ən ˈɒfɪs]	in einem Büro
chef [ʃef]	Koch, Köchin
vet (Abk. v. veterinarian) [vet] [ˌvetrɪˈneərɪən]	Tierarzt, Tierärztin
on a farm [ɒn ə ˈfɑːm]	auf einem Bauernhof
engineer [ˌendʒɪˈnɪə]	Ingenieur/in

3/1B

in the order [ɪn ðɪ ˈɔːdə]	in der Reihenfolge
to play the piano [tʊ pleɪ ðə pɪˈænəʊ]	Klavier spielen
to look after [tʊ lʊk ˈɑːftə]	auf jemanden aufpassen, sich um jemanden kümmern
choir [kwaɪə]	Chor

3/2A

questionnaire [ˌkwestʃəˈneə]	Fragebogen
to have breakfast [tʊ hæv ˈbrekfəst]	frühstücken
to forget [tʊ fəˈget]	vergessen
daily newspaper [ˌdeɪlɪ ˈnjuːzˌpeɪpə]	Tageszeitung

to go shopping [tʊ gəʊ ˈʃɒpɪŋ]	einkaufen gehen
to enjoy [tʊ ɪnˈdʒɔɪ]	genießen, Spaß machen
work [wɜːk]	Arbeit
to go on holiday [tʊ gəʊ ɒn ˈhɒlɪdeɪ]	Urlaub machen
always [ˈɔːlweɪz]	immer
usually [ˈjuːʒəlɪ]	normalerweise
never [ˈnevə]	nie

3/2B

to interview someone [tʊ ˈɪntəvjuː ˌsʌmwʌn]	jemanden interviewen, befragen

3/2C

to tell [tʊ ˈtel]	erzählen

3/3

to have a great time [tʊ hæv ə ˌgreɪt ˈtaɪm]	großartig gefallen

3/3A

boring [ˈbɔːrɪŋ]	langweilig
basic [ˈbeɪsɪk]	einfach
expensive [ɪkˈspensɪv]	teuer
terrible [ˈterəbl]	schrecklich
helpful [ˈhelpfʊl]	hilfsbereit
luxurious [lʌgˈʒʊərɪəs]	luxuriös
cold and rainy [ˌkəʊld ən ˈreɪnɪ]	kalt und regnerisch

3/3B

training course [ˈtreɪnɪŋ ˌkɔːs]	Ausbildungskurs
really [ˈriːlɪ]	wirklich
to stay in a hotel [tʊ ˌsteɪ ɪn ə həʊˈtel]	im Hotel übernachten
very [ˈverɪ]	sehr
internet cafe [ˈɪntənet ˌkæfeɪ]	Internet Café
I'm looking forward to seeing you. [aɪm lʊkɪŋ ˌfɔːwəd tʊ ˈsiːɪŋ juː]	Ich freue mich darauf, dich/euch zu sehen.
regards [rɪˈgɑːdz]	Gruß

3/4A

statistics [stəˈtɪstɪks]	Statistiken
true or false [ˌtruː ɔː ˈfɔːls]	richtig oder falsch
it's a hard life [ɪts ə ˌhɑːd ˈlaɪf]	das Leben ist hart
in any case [ɪn ˈenɪ ˌkeɪs]	auf jeden Fall
to compare [tʊ kəmˈpeə]	vergleichen
working hours [ˈwɜːkɪŋ ˌaʊəz]	Arbeitsstunden

income ['ɪnkʌm] — Einkommen
per day [pə 'deɪ] — pro Tag
average hourly wage — durchschnittlicher
  [ˌævərɪdʒ ˌaʊəlɪ 'weɪdʒ] — Stundenlohn
total income — Gesamteinkommen
  [ˌtəʊtl 'ɪnkʌm]
net income [ˌnet 'ɪnkʌm] — Nettoeinkommen
including public holidays — einschließlich
  [ɪn'kluːdɪŋ ˌpʌblɪk — Feiertage
  'hɒlɪdeɪz]
the most [ðə 'məʊst] — der, die, das meiste
fewer [fjuːə] — weniger
less [les] — weniger

Unit 4 *Revision*

4

letter chain ['letə ˌtʃeɪn] — Buchstabenkette
to create [tʊ krɪ'eɪt] — machen, entwerfen
to think of [tʊ 'θɪŋk əv] — ausdenken
to decode [tʊ ˌdiː'kəʊd] — entschlüsseln
the following message — die folgende
  [ðə ˌfɒləʊɪŋ 'mesɪdʒ] — Nachricht
coded ['kəʊdɪd] — verschlüsselt
to exchange — austauschen
  [tʊ ɪks'tʃeɪndʒ]
to write a reply — eine Antwort
  [tʊ ˌraɪt ə rɪ'plaɪ] — schreiben
to answer the phone — ans Telefon gehen
  [tʊ ˌɑːnsə ðə 'fəʊn]
to throw [tʊ θrəʊ] — werfen
another person — eine andere Person
  [əˌnʌðə 'pɜːsn]
to hold [tʊ həʊld] — halten
until [ən'tɪl] — bis
excuse [ɪks'kjuːs] — Entschuldigung

Unit 5 *Looking Back*

5

to look back [tʊ lʊk 'bæk] — zurückblicken

5/1A

to move to Canada — nach Kanada ziehen
  [tʊ muːv tʊ 'kænədə]
phrase [freɪz] — Wendung
to move [tʊ muːv] — umziehen
removal [rɪ'muːvəl] — Entfernung,
  — Beseitigung
removed [rɪ'muːvd] — entfernt, beseitigt
movement ['muːvmənt] — Bewegung

5/1B

underline [ˌʌndə'laɪn] — unterstreichen Sie
to be born [tʊ bɪ 'bɔːn] — geboren werden

at first [ət 'fɜːst] — zuerst
to miss [tʊ mɪs] — vermissen
soon [suːn] — bald
most of all ['məʊst əv ˌɔːl] — am meisten
to finish college — Studium abschließen
  (BE university)
  [tʊ ˌfɪnɪʃ 'kɒlɪdʒ]
  [tʊ ˌfɪnɪʃ ˌjuːnɪ'vɜːsəti]
to start work with — bei (einer Firma)
  [tʊ stɑːt 'wɜːk wɪð] — anfangen
however [haʊ'evə] — aber, dennoch
three years ago — vor drei Jahren
  [θriː 'jɪəz əˌgəʊ]
to buy [tʊ baɪ] — kaufen
farmhouse ['fɑːmhaʊs] — Bauernhaus
flat [flæt] — Wohnung
to renovate [tʊ 'renəveɪt] — renovieren
to run a business — eine Geschäft
  [tʊ rʌn ə 'bɪznɪs] — betreiben
adult ['ædʌlt] [ə'dʌlt] — Erwachsene/r

5/1C

timeline ['taɪmlaɪn] — Zeitlinie

5/1D

to ask [tʊ ˌɑːsk] — fragen
to answer [tʊ ˌɑːnsə] — antworten,
  — beantworten

5/2

story ['stɔːrɪ] — Geschichte

5/2B

to find out [tʊ faɪnd 'aʊt] — herausfinden

5/2C

to present [tʊ prɪ'zent] — vorstellen,
  — präsentieren
fact [fækt] — Tatsache, Fakt

5/3

business meeting — Geschäfts-
  ['bɪznɪs ˌmiːtɪŋ] — besprechung

5/3A

performance review — Beurteilung
  [pə'fɔːməns rɪˌvjuː]
I have a meeting — ich habe eine
  [aɪ hæv ə 'miːtɪŋ] — Besprechung
he's expecting me — er erwartet mich
  [hiːz ɪk'spektɪŋ miː]
look through — durchsehen
  [lʊk 'θruː]
while I'm waiting — während ich warte
  [waɪl aɪm 'weɪtɪŋ]
Why don't you take — Warum nehmen Sie
  a seat? — nicht Platz?
  [ˌwaɪ dəʊnt jʊ ˌteɪk ə 'siːt]

5/Text

native speaker [ˌneɪtɪv ˈspiːkə] — Muttersprachler/in

exception [ɪkˈsepʃn] — Ausnahme

5/3B

employee [ɪmˈplɔɪiː] — Angestellte/r

purchasing department [ˈpɜːtʃəsɪŋ dɪˌpɑːtmənt] — Einkaufsabteilung

sales department [ˈseɪlz dɪˌpɑːtmənt] — Vertriebsabteilung

slowly [ˈsləʊlɪ] — langsam

independently [ˌɪndɪˈpendəntlɪ] — unabhängig

task [tɑːsk] — Aufgabe

efficiently [ɪˈfɪʃəntlɪ] — effizient

productively [prəˈdʌktɪvlɪ] — produktiv

to be late [tʊ bɪ ˈleɪt] — zu spät sein

effectively [ɪˈfektɪvlɪ] — effektiv

to get on (badly) with someone [tʊ get ˈɒn wɪð ˌsʌmwʌn] [tʊ get ɒn ˈbædlɪ wɪð ˌsʌmwʌn] — mit jemandem (schlecht) auskommen

punctual [ˈpʌŋktʃʊəl] — pünktlich

5/3C

to think carefully about [tʊ θɪŋk ˈkeəfʊlɪ əˌbaʊt] — gründlich darüber nachdenken

future [ˈfjuːtʃə] — Zukunft

Unit 6 *Then and now*

6

then and now [ˌðen ənˈnaʊ] — damals und heute

6/1A

to brainstorm [tʊ ˈbreɪnstɔːm] — gemeinsam erarbeiten

to have [tʊ hæv] — haben

grandparents [ˈɡrændˌpeərənts] — Großeltern

dishwasher [ˈdɪʃˌwɒʃə] — Spülmaschine

6/1B

to have a quiet / busy life [tʊ hæv ə ˌkwaɪət / ˌbɪzɪ ˈlaɪf] — ein ruhiges / arbeitsreiches Leben haben

to grow vegetables [tʊ ɡrəʊ ˈvedʒtəblz] — Gemüse anbauen

to make your own bread [tʊ meɪk jɔːrˌəʊn ˈbred] — sein eigenes Brot backen

to do something by hand [tʊ duː ˌsʌmθɪŋ ˌbaɪ ˈhænd] — etwas von Hand machen

to get around [tʊ get əˈraʊnd] — herumkommen

by bike [baɪ ˈbaɪk] — mit dem Fahrrad

before [bɪˈfɔː] — vor, bevor

bakery [ˈbeɪkərɪ] — Bäckerei

6/Text

religious community [rɪˌlɪdʒəs kəˈmjuːnətɪ] — religiöse Gemeinschaft

mainly [ˈmeɪnlɪ] — hauptsächlich

nearly [ˈnɪəlɪ] — beinahe, fast

the same dialect [ðə seɪm ˈdaɪəlekt] — derselbe Dialekt

old-fashioned way of life [ˌəʊldˈfæʃnd ˌweɪ əv ˈlaɪf] — altmodische Lebensweise

electricity [ˌelɪkˈtrɪsətɪ] — Strom, Elektrizität

to walk [tʊ wɔːk] — zu Fuß gehen

school bus [ˈskuːlbʌs] — Schulbus

to take them there [tʊ ˈteɪk ðəm ˌðeə] — um sie dorthin zu bringen

6/2A

to number [tʊ ˈnʌmbə] — nummerieren

to contact [tʊ ˈkɒntækt] — kontaktieren, sich mit jemandem in Verbindung setzen

to get [tʊ get] — bekommen

fax machine [ˈfæks məˌʃiːn] — Faxgerät

to copy [tʊ ˈkɒpɪ] — kopieren

document [ˈdɒkjəmənt] — Dokument

photocopier [ˈfəʊtəʊˌkɒpɪə] — Fotokopierer

to leave school [tʊ liːv ˈskuːl] — die Schule abschließen

still [stɪl] — noch

6/2B

statement [ˈsteɪtmənt] — Aussage

nowadays [ˈnaʊədeɪz] — heutzutage

in those days [ɪn ˈðəʊz ˌdeɪz] — damals

6/3A

phone conversation [ˈfəʊn kɒnvəˌseɪʃn] — Telefongespräch

yesterday [ˈjestədeɪ] — gestern

nice [naɪs] — schön, nett

suddenly [ˈsʌdənlɪ] — plötzlich

unbelievable [ˌʌnbɪˈliːvəbl] — unglaublich

to turn off [tʊ tɜːn ˈɒf] — ausschalten

public place [ˌpʌblɪk ˈpleɪs] — öffentlicher Ort

especially [ɪˈspeʃəlɪ] — besonders

to be with other people — in Gesellschaft sein
[tʊ bɪ wɪð ˌʌðə 'pi:pl]
safe [seɪf] — sicher
dark [dɑ:k] — dunkel
to look for [tʊ 'lʊk fɔ:] — suchen nach
essential [ɪ'senʃl] — absolut erforderlich /
notwendig

clients ['klaɪənts] — Kunden
emergency [ɪ'mɜ:dʒənsɪ] — Notfall
like last night — wie letzte Nacht
[laɪk ˌlɑ:st 'naɪt]
to make an unplanned — einen nicht
visit — geplanten Besuch
[tʊ meɪk ən ʌnˌplænd 'vɪzɪt] machen
to save time — Zeit sparen
[tʊ seɪv 'taɪm]
mobile (= mobile phone) — Handy
['məʊbaɪl]
bill [bɪl] — Rechnung
to get bigger — größer werden
[tʊ get 'bɪgə]

6/3B
to make appointments — Termine ausmachen
[tʊ meɪk ə'pɔɪntmənts]
to take a photo — ein Bild / Foto
[tʊ teɪk ə 'fəʊtəʊ] machen
to send text messages — SMS verschicken
[tʊ send 'tekst ˌmesɪdʒɪz]

6/4
shelter ['ʃeltə] — Unterstand
to make calls — Telefongespräche
[tʊ meɪk ˌkɔ:lz] führen

6/PS
animal ['ænɪml] — Tier

Unit 7 *Holidays*

7/1A
city break [ˌsɪtɪ 'breɪk] — Städtetour
cruise [kru:z] — Kreuzfahrt
Neither do I. — Ich auch nicht.
[ˌnaɪðə dʊ 'aɪ]
to prefer [tʊ prɪ'fɜ:] — bevorzugen

7/1B
to have to do something — etwas machen
[tʊ hæv tʊ 'du: ˌsʌmθɪŋ] müssen
as many words as — so viele Wörter wie
possible — möglich
[əz ˌmenɪ wɜ:dz əz 'pɒsəbl]
next to ['nekst ˌtʊ] — neben
to book [tʊ bʊk] — buchen

to organize — organisieren
[tʊˌ'ɔ:gənaɪz]
to check [tʊ tʃek] — prüfen
to collect [tʊ kə'lekt] — abholen
to cancel [tʊ 'kænsl] — stornieren,
abbestellen
car rental ['kɑ: ˌrentl] — Autovermietung
suitcase ['su:tkeɪs] — Koffer
sun cream ['sʌnkri:m] — Sonneschutzcreme
dentist's appointment — Zahnarzttermin
['dentɪsts əˌpɔɪntmənt]
travel agent — Reisebürokaufmann/
['trævl ˌeɪdʒənt] frau

7/1C
to pack [tʊ pæk] — packen
passenger ticket — Fluggastticket
['pæsɪndʒə ˌtɪkɪt]
boarding pass — Bordkarte
['bɔ:dɪŋ ˌpɑ:s]
check-in required — Einchecken
[ˌtʃekɪn rɪ'kwaɪəd] erforderlich

7/2A
dental surgery — Zahnarztpraxis
['dentl ˌsɜ:dʒərɪ]
certainly ['sɜ:tənlɪ] — aber sicher, natürlich
we could fit you in — wir könnten Sie
this evening — heute Abend
[wɪ kʊd ˌfɪt jʊ in ðɪs 'i:vnɪŋ] einschieben
Yes, that's fine. — Ja, das geht.
[jes ðæts 'faɪn]
let me check — lassen Sie mich
[ˌlet mɪ 'tʃek] nachsehen
You're welcome. — Gern geschehen.
[jɔ: 'welkʌm]
I can't make Friday — Freitag kann ich nicht
[aɪ ˌkɑ:nt meɪk 'fraɪdeɪ]
check-up ['tʃekʌp] — Routineuntersuchung
Would five thirty be — Passt Ihnen halb
convenient? — sechs?
[wʊd ˌfaɪv 'θɜ:tɪ bɪ
kənˌvi:nɪənt]

7/3
to smile [tʊ smaɪl] — lächeln

7/3A
to note [tʊ nəʊt] — notieren
today [tə'deɪ] — heute
I've been to … — Ich war schon
[aɪv ˌbɪn tʊ]

7/3B
in common [ɪn 'kɒmən] — gemeinsam

7/5A

road trip *(AE)* ['rəʊd ˌtrɪp]	*Tour per Auto oder Wohnmobil durch ein Land/eine Region*
avid ['ævɪd]	begeistert, passioniert
along [ə'lɒŋ]	entlang
route [ruːt]	Route
from coast to coast [frəm ˌkəʊst tʊ 'kəʊst]	von Küste zu Küste
internet site ['ɪntənet ˌsaɪt]	Website
all about [ɔːl ə'baʊt]	alles über
to give advice [tʊ gɪv əd'vaɪs]	Rat geben
general information [ˌdʒenrəl ˌɪnfə'meɪʃn]	allgemeine Informationen
kind of vacation [ˌkaɪnd əv və'keɪʃn]	Art, Urlaub zu machen
motorhome ['məʊtəˌhəʊm]	Wohnmobil
in the time available [ɪn ðə ˌtaɪm ə'veɪləbl]	in der verfügbaren Zeit
to drive [tʊ draɪv]	(Auto) fahren
along the way [əˌlɒŋ ðə 'weɪ]	unterwegs

Unit 8 *Revision*

8

mime an activity [ˌmaɪm ən æk'tɪvəti]	eine Handlung pantomimisch darstellen
the first half [ðə 'fɜːst ˌhɑːf]	die erste Hälfte
to guess [tʊ ges]	raten
to add [tʊ ˌæd]	hinzufügen
to try [tʊ traɪ]	versuchen
to tell a story [tʊ tel ə 'stɔːri]	eine Geschichte erzählen
a piece of paper [ə ˌpiːs əv 'peɪpə]	ein Blatt Papier
to draw [tʊ drɔː]	zeichnen
to describe [tʊ dɪ'skraɪb]	beschreiben
to translate [tʊ trænz'leɪt]	übersetzen

Unit 9 *A trip down under*

9

a trip down under [ə 'trɪp ˌdaʊn'ʌndə]	eine Reise nach Australien

9/Text

Aboriginal [ˌæbə'rɪdʒənl]	der australischen Ureinwohner
local ['ləʊkl]	einheimisch

9/1A

map [mæp]	Landkarte
about 1000 km up the coast [əˌbaʊt ə 'θaʊzənd kɪˌlɒmɪtəz ʌp ðə 'kəʊst]	ungefähr 1000 km die Küste hinauf
to take a boat trip [tʊ teɪk ə 'bəʊt ˌtrɪp]	einen Bootsausflug machen
to travel across the Outback [tʊ ˌtrævl əˌkrɒs ðɪ 'aʊtbæk]	quer durch das (australische) Hinterland fahren
we're leaving the motorhome [wɪə ˌliːvɪŋ ðə 'məʊtəˌhəʊm]	wir geben das Wohnmobil ab
railway ['reɪlweɪ]	Eisenbahn
to arrive [tʊ ə'raɪv]	ankommen
to sightsee [tʊ 'saɪtsiː]	besichtigen
we're going to the opera [wɪə ˌgəʊɪŋ tʊ ðɪ 'ɒprə]	wir gehen in die Oper

9/1B

means of transport [ˌmiːnz əv 'trænspɔːt]	Beförderungsmittel

9/1C

let's take the Indian Pacific ['lets teɪk ðɪˌɪndɪən pə'sɪfɪk]	lasst uns mit dem Indian Pacific fahren
Why don't we go hiking? [ˌwaɪ dəʊnt wi gəʊ 'haɪkɪŋ]	Warum gehen wir nicht wandern?

9/2A

kitchen area ['kɪtʃɪn ˌeərɪə]	Küchenbereich
dining area ['daɪnɪŋ ˌeərɪə]	Essbereich
living area ['lɪvɪŋ ˌeərɪə]	Wohnbereich
table ['teɪbl]	Tisch
A/C (air conditioning) [ˌeɪ'siː] ['eə kənˌdɪʃənɪŋ]	Klimaanlage
wardrobe ['wɔːdrəʊb]	Kleiderschrank
wash basin ['wɒʃ ˌbeɪsn]	Waschbecken
shower [ʃaʊə]	Dusche
fridge [frɪdʒ]	Kühlschrank
stove [stəʊv]	Herd
overhead microwave [ˌəʊvəhed 'maɪkrəʊweɪv]	an der Wand ange- brachte Mikrowelle

cupboard ['kʌbəd]	Schrank	
step [step]	Stufe	

9/2B

advert ['ædvɜ:t]	Anzeige
to recommend [tʊ ˌrekəˈmend]	empfehlen
to convert [tʊ kənˈvɜ:t]	sich umbauen lassen
a large double bed [ə lɑ:dʒ ˌdʌbl ˈbed]	ein großes Doppelbett
to include [tʊ ɪnˈklu:d]	einschließen, enthalten
chair [tʃeə]	Stuhl
spacious ['speɪʃəs]	geräumig
plenty of storage space [ˌplentɪ ˌəv ˈstɔ:rɪdʒ ˌspeɪs]	viel Stauraum
to accommodate up to [tʊ əˈkɒmədeɪt ʌp tu:]	Platz für bis zu (4 Personen) bieten
standard equipment [ˌstændəd ɪˈkwɪpmənt]	Standardausstattung
freezer ['fri:zə]	Gefrierfach, Gefrierschrank
crockery and cutlery [ˌkrɒkərɪ ˌən ˈkʌtlərɪ]	Geschirr und Besteck
cooking utensils ['kʊkɪŋ juːˌtenslz]	Kochutensilien
personal details [ˌpɜ:sənl ˈdi:teɪlz]	Personalien
No. (number) ['nʌmbə]	Nr. (Nummer)
approximately (approx.) [əˈprɒksɪmətlɪ]	ungefähr, circa (ca.)
to pick up someone / something [tʊ pɪk ˈʌp ˌsʌmwʌn / ˌsʌmθɪŋ]	jemanden / etwas abholen
to drop off someone / something [tʊ drɒp ˈɒf ˌsʌmwʌn / ˌsʌmθɪŋ]	jemanden absetzen, etwas abliefern
additional [əˈdɪʃənl]	zusätzlich
road atlas ['rəʊd ˌætləs]	Straßenatlas

9/2C

I'd like to make a booking. [aɪd laɪk tʊ ˌmeɪk ə ˈbʊkɪŋ]	Ich möchte eine Buchung machen.
so that's [səʊ ˈðæts]	(hier) das wäre
until [ənˈtɪl]	bis
Yes, that's right. [jes ˌðæts ˈraɪt]	Ja, das stimmt.
all inclusive [ˌɔ:l ɪnˈklu:sɪv]	alles inklusive

9/3A

to make sure [tʊ meɪk ˈʃɔ:]	darauf achten

to watch out [tʊ wɒtʃ ˈaʊt]	sich in Acht nehmen
to wear a seat belt [tʊ weəˌə ˈsi:tˌbelt]	einen Sicherheitsgurt tragen
driving licence ['draɪvɪŋ ˌlaɪsəns]	Führerschein
valid ['vælɪd]	gültig
enough petrol [ɪˌnʌf ˈpetrəl]	genügend Benzin

9/PS

I can come and see you [aɪ kən ˌkʌm ən ˈsi: ju:]	ich kann dich besuchen kommen
instead [ɪnˈsted]	anstatt
per 100 kilometres [pə ˌhʌndrəd kɪˈlɒmɪtəz]	pro 100 Kilometer
sunglasses ['sʌnˌglɑ:sɪz]	Sonnenbrille
in total [ɪn ˈtəʊtl]	insgesamt

Unit 10 *Eating out*

10

eating out [ˌi:tɪŋ ˈaʊt]	auswärts essen

10/1

How about Indian? [haʊ əˌbaʊt ˈɪndɪən]	Wie wäre es mit Indisch?
atmosphere ['ætməsfɪə]	Atmosphäre, Stimmung
till late [tɪlˌˈleɪt]	bis spät
taste [teɪst]	Geschmack
fully licensed [ˌfʊlɪ ˈlaɪsənst]	mit Schankerlaubnis
Thai cuisine [ˌtaɪ kwɪzˈi:n]	thailändische Küche
takeaway ['teɪkəweɪ]	Gericht zum Mitnehmen
delivery [dɪˈlɪvərɪ]	Lieferung nach Haus
seafood ['si:fu:d]	Meeresfrüchte
inside or outside [ˌɪnsaɪd ɔ:rˈˈaʊtsaɪd]	drinnen oder draußen
relaxed dining [rɪˌlækst ˈdaɪnɪŋ]	Speisen in entspannter Atmosphäre
overlooking the harbour [ˌəʊvəlʊkɪŋ ðə ˈhɑ:bə]	mit Blick auf den Hafen
exotic [ɪgˈzɒtɪk]	exotisch

10/1A

to take home [tʊ teɪk ˈhəʊm]	mit nach Hause nehmen
to go out for dinner [tʊ gəʊˌaʊt fə ˈdɪnə]	Abends essen gehen

10/2A

lovely ['lʌvlɪ]	schön, wunderbar
delicious [dɪˈlɪʃəs]	köstlich

really tasty [ˌriːlɪ ˈteɪstɪ]	sehr lecker	capital [ˈkæpɪtl]	Hauptstadt
all in all [ˌɔːl ɪn ˈɔːl]	alles in allem	per head [pə ˈhed]	pro Kopf
excellent value for money [ˈeksələnt ˌvæljuː fə ˈmʌnɪ]	das Geld wert	vineyard [ˈvɪnjɑːd]	Weingut, Weinberg
		a third [ə ˈθɜːd]	ein Drittel
		to produce [tʊ prəˈdjuːs]	produzieren
service [ˈsɜːvɪs]	Bedienung	to export [tʊˌɪkˈspɔːt]	exportieren

10/2B

poor [pɔː]	schlecht
tasteless [ˈteɪstləs]	wenig schmackhaft, fade

10/2C

recently [ˈriːsəntlɪ]	neulich

10/3

menu [ˈmenjuː]	Speisekarte
starter [ˈstɑːtə]	Vorspeise
ham [hæm]	Schinken
garlic [ˈgɑːlɪk]	Knoblauch
soup [suːp]	Suppe
main course [ˌmeɪn ˈkɔːs]	Hauptgericht
beef [biːf]	Rind
sweet [swiːt]	süß
very spicy [ˌverɪ ˈspaɪsɪ]	sehr würzig
smoked salmon [ˌsməʊkt ˈsæmən]	Räucherlachs
baked potato [ˌbeɪkt pəˈteɪtəʊ]	Folienkartoffel
artichoke [ˈɑːtɪtʃəʊk]	Artischocke
onion [ˈʌnjən]	Zwiebel
prawns [prɔːnz]	Garnelen
mussels [ˈmʌslz]	Muscheln
shrimps [ʃrɪmps]	Schrimps
chicken [ˈtʃɪkɪn]	Huhn
mushroom [ˈmʌʃruːm]	Champignon
vegetarian pasta [vedʒəˌteərɪən ˈpæstə]	vegetarisches Nudelgericht
basil [ˈbæzl]	Basilikum
side salad [ˈsaɪd ˌsæləd]	Salatbeilage
dessert [dɪˈzɜːt]	Dessert, Nachtisch
kiwifruit [ˈkiːwiːˌfruːt]	Kiwi
mint sauce [ˌmɪnt ˈsɔːs]	Minzsoße
service is included [ˌsɜːvɪs ɪz ɪnˈkluːdɪd]	Bedienung inklusive

10/3A

meat [miːt]	Fleisch
fruit [fruːt]	Obst
herbs and spices [ˌhɜːbz ən ˈspaɪsɪz]	Kräuter und Gewürze
dairy product [ˈdeərɪ ˌprɒdʌkt]	Milchprodukt

10/Text

food and drink [ˌfuːd ən ˈdrɪŋk]	Essen und Trinken

10/4A

Are you ready to order? [ɑː jʊ ˌredɪ tʊˌˈɔːdə]	Sind Sie soweit?
the Laksa is off [ðə ˌlæksərˌɪz ˈɒf]	das Laksa ist aus
instead of [ɪnˈsted əv]	anstatt, anstelle
certainly [ˈsɜːtənlɪ]	aber natürlich, selbstverständlich
Anything else? [ˌenɪθɪŋ ˈels]	Sonst noch etwas?
without [wɪˈðaʊt]	ohne
local wines [ˌləʊkl ˈwaɪnz]	Weine aus der Umgebung
I'll just go and check. [aɪl ˌdʒʌst gəʊˌən ˈtʃek]	Ich sehe gerade einmal nach.

Unit 11 *Health and Body*

11

health and body [ˌhelθ ən ˈbɒdɪ]	Gesundheit und Körper

11/1

body and soul [ˌbɒdɪˌən ˈsəʊl]	Körper und Seele

11/1A

appropriate [əˈprəʊprɪət]	geeignet, passend
to play [tʊ pleɪ]	spielen
gym [dʒɪm]	Fitnessstudio

11/1B

of the above [əv ðɪ əˈbʌv]	von den oben genannten/obigen
regularly [ˈregjələlɪ]	regelmäßig

11/1C

to keep fit [tʊ kiːp ˈfɪt]	sich fit halten
healthy [ˈhelθɪ]	gesund
once [wʌns]	einmal
twice [twaɪs]	zweimal
three times [ˌθriː ˈtaɪmz]	dreimal

11/1D

to do yoga [tʊ ˌduː ˈjəʊgə]	Yoga machen

11/2A

body parts [ˈbɒdɪ ˌpɑːts]	Körperteile

I feel terrible
[aɪ fiːl 'terəbl]
ich fühle mich schrecklich

to have a headache
[tʊ hæv ə 'hedeɪk]
Kopfschmerzen haben

in fact [ɪn 'fækt]
in der Tat

my whole body aches
[maɪ ˌhəʊl 'bɒdɪˌeɪks]
mein ganzer Körper schmerzt / tut mir weh

to have a sore throat
[tʊ hæv ə ˌsɔː 'θrəʊt]
Halsschmerzen haben

my nose is running
[maɪ 'nəʊz ɪz ˌrʌnɪŋ]
meine Nase läuft

flu (Abk. v. influenza)
[fluː] [ˌɪnflʊ'enzə]
Grippe

I'm just stressed
[aɪm ˌdʒʌst 'strest]
ich bin nur gestresst

I broke my foot
[aɪ ˌbrəʊk maɪ 'fʊt]
ich habe mir den Fuß gebrochen

11/2B

illness ['ɪlnəs]
Krankheit

common health complaint
[ˌkɒmən 'helθ kəmˌpleɪnt]
häufige Gesundheits-beschwerden

11/2C

ill [ɪl]
krank

remedy ['remədɪ]
Heilmittel

throat sweets
['θrəʊt ˌswiːts]
Halsbonbons

11/3A

energy ['enədʒɪ]
Energie, Kraft

technique [tek'niːk]
Methode, Technik

to be affected by stress
[tʊ bɪˌəˌfektɪd baɪ 'stres]
unter Stress stehen

to reduce [tʊ rɪ'djuːs]
reduzieren, abbauen

a few ways [ə fjuː 'weɪz]
einige Wege

caffeine ['kæfiːn]
Koffein

to be physically active
[tʊ bɪ ˌfɪzɪklɪ'æktɪv]
körperlich aktiv sein

to do sport [tʊ duː 'spɔːt]
Sport treiben

they may be able to help you
[ðeɪ meɪ bɪˌˌeɪbl tʊ 'help juː]
sie könnten Ihnen möglicherweise helfen

to try [tʊ traɪ]
ausprobieren, es versuchen mit

relaxation [ˌriːlæk'seɪʃn]
Entspannung

11/3C

with your back straight
[wɪð jɔː ˌbæk 'streɪt]
mit geradem Rücken

Lift your right leg.
[ˌlɪft jɔː ˌraɪt 'leg]
Heben Sie Ihr rechtes Bein.

Point your toes.
[ˌpɔɪnt jɔː 'təʊz]
Strecken Sie Ihre Zehen.

Repeat with your left leg.
[rɪˌpiːt wɪð jɔː ˌleft 'leg]
Wiederholen Sie (die Übung) mit Ihrem linken Bein.

Pull your foot back.
[ˌpʊl jɔː 'fʊt ˌbæk]
Ziehen Sie den Fuß an.

Pull your shoulder blades together.
[ˌpʊl jɔː 'ʃəʊldə ˌbleɪdz təˌgeðə]
Ziehen Sie die Schulterblätter zusammen.

Raise your arms.
[ˌreɪz jɔːr 'ɑːmz]
Heben Sie Ihre Arme (an).

Stretch as high as you can.
[ˌstretʃ əz ˌhaɪˌəz juː 'kæn]
Strecken Sie sich so hoch Sie können.

Close your eyes.
[ˌkləʊz jɔːr 'aɪz]
Machen Sie Ihre Augen zu.

Take a deep breath.
[ˌteɪk ə 'diːp ˌbreθ]
Atmen Sie tief ein.

Breathe out slowly.
[ˌbriːð aʊt 'sləʊlɪ]
Atmen Sie langsam aus.

11/4

whatever the weather
[wɒtˌevə ðə 'weðə]
ganz gleich wie das Wetter ist

11/4A

season ['siːzn]
Jahreszeit

snow [snəʊ]
Schnee

showers [ʃaʊəz]
(Regen)schauer

thunderstorm
['θʌndəstɔːm]
Gewitter

cloudy ['klaʊdɪ]
wolkig, bewölkt

foggy ['fɒgɪ]
neblig

dry [draɪ]
trocken

11/4B

clothes [kləʊðz]
Kleidung

normally ['nɔːməlɪ]
normalerweise

gloves [glʌvz]
Handschuhe

boots [buːts]
Stiefel

dress [dres]
Kleid

skirt [skɜːt]
Rock

scarf [skɑːf]
Schal

coat [kəʊt]
Mantel

11/4C

weekly ['wiːklɪ]
wöchentlich

weather report
['weðə rɪˌpɔːt]
Wetterbericht

sunshine ['sʌnʃaɪn]
Sonnenschein

sunny periods
[ˌsʌnɪ 'pɪərɪədz]
sonnige Abschnitte

11/4D

if [ɪf]
wenn, falls

11/PS

finally ['faɪməlɪ]	zuletzt, schließlich
temperatures around 32°C (centigrade) [ˌtemprətʃəz əraʊnd ˌθɜːtɪ ˈtuː dɪˌɡriːz ˈsentɪɡreɪd]	Temperaturen um die 32 Grad
shoulder ['ʃəʊldə]	Schulter
ear [ɪə]	Ohr
neck [nek]	Hals
mouth [maʊθ]	Mund
knee [niː]	Knie
eye [aɪ]	Auge

Unit 12 *Revision*

12

to choose [tʊ tʃuːz]	wählen, auswählen
stand in a circle [ˌstænd ɪn ə ˈsɜːkl]	stellen Sie sich im Kreis auf
someone else [ˌsʌmwʌn ˈels]	jemand anders
to catch [tʊ kætʃ]	fangen
continue [kən'tɪnjuː]	machen Sie weiter
a simple health problem [ə ˌsɪmpl ˈhelθ ˌprɒbləm]	ein einfaches gesund- heitliches Problem
to stick [tʊ stɪk]	kleben
on the back [ɒn ðə ˈbæk]	auf den Rücken
the others give you advice [ðɪ ˌʌðəz ɡɪv jʊ ˌəd'vaɪs]	die anderen geben Ihnen (einen) Rat
rule [ruːl]	Regel
to pass [tʊ pɑːs]	weitergeben
neighbour ['neɪbə]	Nachbar
to get your own paper back [tʊ get jɔːr ˈəʊn ˌpeɪpə ˈbæk]	sein eigenes Blatt zurückerhalten

Unit 13 *Places*

13/1A

village ['vɪlɪdʒ]	Dorf
in the country [ɪn ðə ˈkʌntrɪ]	auf dem Land
mountain ['maʊntɪn]	Berg
sea [siː]	Meer
river ['rɪvə]	Fluss
hill [hɪl]	Hügel

13/1B

about [ə'baʊt]	ungefähr
quite a long way [ˌkwaɪt ə lɒŋˌ'weɪ]	ziemlich weit
on route 2 [ɒn ˌruːtˌ'tuː]	an der Straße 2

13/1D

by the window [baɪ ðə ˈwɪndəʊ]	am Fenster

13/2

How do I get there? [ˌhaʊ dʊˌaɪ ˈgetˌðeə]	Wie komme ich dorthin?
P + R (Abk. v. Park and Ride) [ˌpɑːk ən ˈraɪd]	Park-and-ride-System
to avoid the traffic jams [tʊˌəˌvɔɪd ðə ˈtræfɪk ˌdʒæmz]	die Verkehrsstaus vermeiden
the tube [ðə ˈtjuːb]	die Londoner U-Bahn
take it easy [ˌteɪk ɪt ˈiːzɪ]	nehmen Sie es leicht
the heart of London [ðə ˌhɑːt əv ˈlʌndən]	das Herz Londons
in a new light [ɪn ə ˌnjuː ˈlaɪt]	in einem neuen Licht
to get on [tʊ get ˈɒn]	einsteigen
to discover London [tʊ dɪˈskʌvə ˈlʌndən]	London entdecken
by underground [baɪ ˈʌndəɡraʊnd]	mit der U-Bahn
to change [tʊ tʃeɪndʒ]	umsteigen
to get off [tʊ get ˈɒf]	aussteigen
all day [ˌɔːl ˈdeɪ]	den ganzen Tag

13/2A

to locate [tʊ ləʊ'keɪt]	ausfindig machen

13/2C

note [nəʊt]	Notiz
towards [tə'wɔːdz]	Richtung

13/2D

excuse me [ɪk'skjuːz ˌmiː]	entschuldigen Sie bitte

13/3

lost and found [ˌlɒst ən ˈfaʊnd]	Fundbüro

13/3A

I've left my umbrella [aɪv left maɪˌʌm'brelə]	ich habe meinen Regenschirm liegen lassen
change [tʃeɪndʒ]	Kleingeld
ticket machine ['tɪkɪt məˌʃiːn]	Fahrkartenautomat
someone has stolen my purse [ˌsʌmwʌn hæzˌstəʊln maɪ 'pɜːs]	man hat mir mein Portemonnaie gestohlen
lost property office [ˌlɒst 'prɒpətɪˌɒfɪs]	Fundbüro

don't worry ['dəʊnt ˌwʌrɪ]   keine Sorge
debit card ['debɪtˌkɑːd]   Kundenkarte

13/4
changes ['tʃeɪndʒɪz]   Veränderungen

13/4A
sooner ['suːnə]   eher
busy ['bɪzɪ]   beschäftigt
since [sɪns]   seit, seitdem
to change [tʊ tʃeɪndʒ]   (ver)ändern
They've finished the new metro line.   Sie haben die neue Stadtbahnlinie fertiggestellt.
   [ðeɪ ˌfɪnɪʃt ðə njuː 'metrəʊ ˌlaɪn]
directly into the city   direkt in die Stadt
   [dɪˌrektlɪ ˌɪntʊ ðə 'sɪtɪ]
as part of her Golden Jubilee   im Rahmen Ihres Goldenen Jubiläums
   [əz ˌpɑːt əv hɜː ˌgəʊldən 'dʒuːbɪliː]
they've built a roof   sie haben ein Dach gebaut
   [ðeɪv bɪlt ə 'ruːf]
over the whole high street   über die ganze Hauptstraße
   [ˌəʊvə ðə ˌhəʊl 'haɪ ˌstriːt]
like a wind tunnel   wie ein Windkanal
   [laɪk ə 'wɪndˌtʌnl]
paths for walkers and cyclists   Wander- und Radwege
   ['pɑːðz fə ˌwɔːkəz ənd 'saɪklɪsts]
artists have created sculptures and pictures   Künstler haben Skulpturen und Bilder erschaffen
   [ˌɑːtɪsts həv krɪ'eɪtɪd ˌskʌlptʃəz ənd 'pɪktʃəz]
history ['hɪstərɪ]   Geschichte
coffee shop ['kɒfɪ ˌʃɒp]   Café
not at all [nɒt ət 'ɔːl]   überhaupt nicht
to hope [tʊ həʊp]   hoffen
take care [ˌteɪk ˈkeə]   mach's gut

13/4C
to imagine [tʊ ɪ'mædʒɪn]   sich vorstellen
home town ['həʊm ˌtaʊn]   Heimatstadt

13/Text
Blinking Eye [ˌblɪŋkɪŋ 'aɪ]   Zwinkerndes Auge
which crosses the river   über den Fluss
   [wɪtʃ ˌkrɒsɪz ðə 'rɪvə]
bridge [ˌbrɪdʒ]   Brücke
to move up [tʊ muːv 'ʌp]   hochklappen
ship [ʃɪp]   Schiff
to pass under   unter durchfahren
   [tʊ pɑːs 'ʌndə]
to look like [tʊ 'lʊk laɪk]   aussehen wie

13/PS
colleague ['kɒliːg]   Kollege, Kollegin
indoor swimming pool   Hallenbad
   [ˌɪndɔː 'swɪmɪŋ ˌpuːl]
industrial area   Industriegebiet
   [ɪn'dʌstrɪəl ˌeərɪə]
historical buildings   historische Gebäude
   [hɪˌstɒrɪkl 'bɪldɪŋz]
to enclose [tʊˌɪn'kləʊz]   beifügen
blocks of flats   Wohnblöcke
   [ˌblɒks əv 'flæts]
we graduated from university   wir haben das Studium abgeschlossen
   [wi: 'grædjuˌeɪtɪd frəm juːnɪ'vɜːsətɪ]

Unit 14 *Shopping*

14/1
classifieds ['klæsɪfaɪdz]   Kleinanzeigen
pet [pet]   Haustier
skunk [skʌŋk]   Stinktier
purchase ['pɜːtʃəs]   Kauf, Erwerb
cage [keɪdʒ]   Käfig
house-trained   stubenrein
   ['haʊstreɪnd]
low mileage   niedriger Meilenstand
   [ˌləʊ 'maɪlɪdʒ]
groceries ['grəʊsərɪz]   Lebensmittel
to make payable to   auf jemanden ausstellen
   [tʊ meɪk 'peɪəbl tuː]

14/1A
to shop [tʊ ʃɒp]   einkaufen
item ['aɪtəm]   Artikel
table ['teɪbl]   Tisch
below [bɪ'ləʊ]   unten
cheap flight [ˌtʃiːp 'flaɪt]   Billigflug
second-hand   gebraucht
   [ˌsekənd'hænd]

14/1B
cash [kæʃ]   Bargeld
I pay by cheque / credit card   Ich zahle mit Scheck / Kreditkarte
   [aɪ ˌpeɪ baɪ 'tʃek / 'kredɪt ˌkɑːd]

14/2A
sales assistant   Verkäufer/in
   ['seɪlz əˌsɪstənt]
Is that all?   Ist das alles? Sonst noch ein Wunsch?
   [ɪz ðæt 'ɔːl]
to accept cheques   Schecks nehmen
   [tʊˌək'sept 'tʃeks]

to wrap [tʊ ræp]   (als Geschenk) einpacken

to sign [tʊ saɪn]   unterschreiben
store card ['stɔː ˌkɑːd]   Kundenkarte
I'm just looking.   Ich sehe mich nur um.
[aɪm ˌdʒʌst 'lʊkɪŋ]

14/2C
Do you have any black   Haben Sie schwarze
gloves?   Handschuhe?
[dʊ jʊ hæv enɪ ˌblæk ˈglʌvz]
we don't have any in   wir haben keine in
black   Schwarz
[wɪ ˌdəʊnt hæv ˌenɪ ɪn
'blæk]
we have some in blue   wir haben welche in
[wɪ ˌhæv sʌm ɪn 'bluː]   Blau
receipt [rɪ'siːt]   Kassenzettel,
Quittung

14/3A
order form ['ɔːdə ˌfɔːm]   Bestellformular
are made to the highest   genügt höchsten
standards   Ansprüchen
[ɑː meɪd ˌtʊ ðə 'haɪst
ˌstændədz]
top quality materials   Material von
['tɒp ˌkwɒlətɪ mə'tɪərɪəlz]   Spitzenqualität
to use [tʊ juːz]   verwenden
your satisfaction is   Ihre Zufriedenheit
guaranteed   wird garantiert
[jɔː ˌsætɪs'fækʃn ɪz
ˌgærən'tiːd]
round coffee table   runder Couchtisch
[ˌraʊnd 'kɒfɪ ˌteɪbl]
(is) made of solid wood   aus Vollholz
[ɪz ˌmeɪd əv ˌsɒlɪd 'wʊd]
stylish ['staɪlɪʃ]   stilvoll
metal base [ˌmetəl 'beɪs]   Metallfuß
delivery address   Lieferadresse
[dɪ'lɪvərɪ əˌdres]
quantity ['kwɒntətɪ]   Menge
checkout ['tʃekaʊt]   Kasse

14/3B
I'll put you through   ich verbinde Sie
[aɪl ˌpʊt jʊ 'θruː]
glass top [ˌglɑːs 'tɒp]   Glasplatte

14/3C
the line is busy   die Leitung ist
[ðə ˌlaɪn ɪz 'bɪzɪ]   besetzt
Would you like to hold?   Möchten Sie am
[wʊd jʊ ˌlaɪk tʊ 'həʊld]   Apparat bleiben?

14/Text
two thirds [ˌtuː 'θɜːdz]   zwei drittel

internet user ['ɪntənet   Internetnutzer
ˌjuːzə]
worldwide [ˌwɜːld'waɪd]   weltweit
online ['ɒnlaɪn]   online
three quarters   drei viertel
[ˌθriː 'kwɔːtəz]
beauty products   Schönheitsprodukte
['bjuːtɪ ˌprɒdʌkts]
to make a reservation   eine Reservierung
[tʊ meɪk ə ˌrezə'veɪʃn]   vornehmen
they like to try them   sie möchten sie
on first   zuerst anprobieren
[ðeɪ laɪk tʊ ˌtraɪ ðəm
ˌɒn 'fɜːst]
to be worried about   sich Sorgen um etwas
[tʊ bɪ 'wʌrɪd əˌbaʊt]   machen
security [sɪ'kjʊərətɪ]   Sicherheit

14/4
High-tech lives   Hightechleben
[ˌhaɪtek 'laɪvz]

14/4A
hermit ['hɜːmɪt]   Eremit/in,
Einsiedler/in
working from home   Arbeiten von zu
[ˌwɜːkɪŋ frəm 'həʊm]   Hause aus
to go out [tʊ gəʊˈaʊt]   weggehen, ausgehen
to chat with the   mit den Nachbarn
neighbours   plaudern
[tʊ tʃæt wɪð ðə 'neɪbəz]
to spend time   Zeit verbringen
[tʊ spend ˈtaɪm]
commuting to work   zur Arbeit pendeln
[kəˌmjuːtɪŋ tʊ ˈwɜːk]
to have to [tʊ 'hæv tuː]   müssen
all kinds of [ɔːl 'kaɪndz əv]   alle möglichen
home office [ˌhəʊm 'ɒfɪs]   Büro zu Hause
no longer [nəʊ 'lɒŋgə]   nicht mehr
my biggest worry   meine größte Sorge
[maɪ 'bɪgɪst ˌwʌrɪ]
I have to limit myself   ich muss mich
[aɪ hæv ˌtʊ 'lɪmɪt maɪˌself]   beschränken
I can get other things   ich kann andere
done   Dinge erledigen
[aɪ kən get 'ʌðə θɪŋz ˌdʌn]
to hate [tʊ heɪt]   hassen
agreeable [ə'griːəbl]   angenehm
to wait in queues   Schlange stehen
[tʊˌweɪt ɪn 'kjuːz]
delivered to my door   an die Haustür
[dɪˌlɪvəd ˌtʊ maɪ 'dɔː]   geliefert bekommen
I have become   ich bin geworden
[aɪ hæv bɪ'kʌm]
except I am not alone   aber ich bin nicht
[ɪkˌsept aɪ æm ˌnɒt ə'ləʊn]   allein
cyber space ['saɪbəspeɪs]   Cyberspace

to be in a hurry [tʊ bɪˌɪn ə ˈhʌrɪ]	es eilig haben
to meet people [tʊ ˈmiːt ˌpiːpl]	Leute kennen lernen
to make friends [tʊ meɪk ˈfrendz]	Freunde finden
to play games [tʊ pleɪ ˈɡeɪmz]	Spiele spielen
to look for jobs [tʊ lʊk fə ˈdʒɒbz]	Stellen / Jobs suchen

14/PS

pullover [ˈpʊləʊvə]	Pullover

Unit 15 *Social events*

15/1A

invitation [ˌɪnvɪˈteɪʃn]	Einladung
to wear [tʊ weə]	tragen
evening suit [ˈiːvnɪŋ ˌsuːt]	Smoking
fancy dress costume [ˌfænsɪ ˈdres ˌkɒstjuːm]	(Masken)kostüm
tie [taɪ]	Krawatte
swimming costume [ˈswɪmɪŋ ˌkɒstjuːm]	Badeanzug
dinner dance [ˈdɪnə ˌdɑːns]	Abendessen mit Tanz
fancy dress party [ˌfænsɪ ˈdres ˌpɑːtɪ]	Kostümparty
leaving party [ˈliːvɪŋ ˌpɑːtɪ]	Abschiedsfeier
barbecue [ˈbɑːbɪkjuː]	Grillparty
house-warming party [ˈhaʊsˌwɔːmɪŋ ˌpɑːtɪ]	Einweihungsparty

15/1B

expression [ɪkˈspreʃn]	Ausdruck
to invite [tuˌɪnˈvaɪt]	einladen
formal [ˈfɔːml]	formell
informal [ɪnˈfɔːml]	informell
to reply [tʊ rɪˈplaɪ]	(be)antworten
the directors [ðə dɪˈrektəz]	die Geschäftsführer
to request the pleasure of the company of [tʊ rɪˌkwestˌðə ˌpleʒərˌɒv ðə ˈkʌmpənɪˌɒv]	herzlich einladen
the opening [ðiˈəʊpnɪŋ]	Eröffnung
branch [brɑːntʃ]	Zweigstelle
R.S.V.P. [ˌɑːresviːˈpiː]	um Antwort wird gebeten
Let's party! [ˌlets ˈpɑːtɪ]	Lasst uns feiern!
come along [ˌkʌm əˈlɒŋ]	kommt vorbei
community beach [kəˈmjuːnətɪ ˌbiːtʃ]	Gemeindestrand

bring a bottle [ˌbrɪŋ ə ˈbɒtl]	bringt etwas zum Trinken mit
sandcastle competition [ˈsændˌkɑːsl ˌkɒmpəˈtɪʃn]	Sandburgenwett-bewerb
See you there! [ˌsiː jʊ ˈðeə]	Bis dann!

15/1C

wedding [ˈwedɪŋ]	Hochzeit

15/2A

casual clothes [ˌkæʒʊəl ˈkləʊðz]	Freizeitkleidung
outfit [ˈaʊtfɪt]	Kleidung
What time should I get there? [wɒtˌtaɪm ʃʊd aɪ ˈɡetˌðeə]	Um wie viel Uhr soll ich hingehen?
a written reply [ə ˌrɪtn rɪˈplaɪ]	eine schriftliche Antwort
a small snack [ə ˌsmɔːl ˈsnæk]	ein kleiner Imbiss
meal [miːl]	Mahlzeit

15/3A

to socialise [tʊ ˈsəʊʃəlaɪz]	sich unterhalten
small talk [ˈsmɔːl ˌtɔːk]	Smalltalk, oberfläch-liche Konversation
I sit on my own [aɪ ˌsɪt ɒn maɪˈəʊn]	ich sitze allein
in a corner [ɪn ə ˈkɔːnə]	in einer Ecke
topic [ˈtɒpɪk]	Thema
hopefully [ˈhəʊpfʊlɪ]	hoffentlich
Good luck! [ˌɡʊd ˈlʌk]	Viel Glück!

15/3B

latest [ˈleɪtɪst]	neueste
area [ˈeərɪə]	Gegend
managing director [ˌmænɪdʒɪŋ dɪˈrektə]	Geschäftsführer
wonderful [ˈwʌndəfʊl]	wunderbar, toll
our latest product [aʊə ˌleɪtɪst ˈprɒdʌkt]	unser neuestes Produkt
What's she like? [ˌwɒtsˌʃɪ ˈlaɪk]	Wie ist sie (so)?
Oh really? [ˌəʊ ˈriːlɪ]	Ach wirklich?

15/3D

salary [ˈsælərɪ]	Gehalt
the economy [ðɪˈkɒnəmɪ]	die Wirtschaft

thank-you letter
['θæŋkju: ˌletə]

Dankesbrief

it was very kind of you
[ɪt wəz ˌverɪ 'kaɪnd əv ju:]

es war sehr nett von Ihnen

I hope we shall see each other again soon.
[aɪ ˌhəʊp wɪ ʃəl ˌsi: ˌi:tʃ 'ʌðərˌəˌɡeɪn 'su:n]

Ich hoffe, wir werden uns bald wieder sehen.

very best wishes
[ˌverɪ best 'wɪʃɪz]

mit den allerbesten Wünschen

Unit 16 *Revision*

as quickly as possible
[əz ˌkwɪklɪˌəz 'pɒsəbl]

so schnell wie möglich

on your right / left
[ɒn jɔ: 'raɪt / 'left]

zu Ihrer Rechten / Linken

to keep the conversation going [tʊ ki:p ðə ˌkɒnvə'seɪʃn ˌɡəʊɪŋ]

das Gespräch in Gang halten

for a while [fərˌə 'waɪl]

für eine Weile

one side of a dialogue
[ˌwʌn saɪd əv ə 'daɪəlɒɡ]

eine Seite eines Dialogs

read along [ˌri:d ə'lɒŋ]

lesen Sie mit

Alphabetical Word List
Alphabetisches Wortregister

Die Wörter sind hier in alphabetischer Reihenfolge aufgelistet und mit einer Verweisnummer versehen, z.B. 1/1B (Unit 1, Teil 1, Übung B).
Verwiesen wird jeweils auf das erste Vorkommen des Wortes im Buch.

(AE) = amerikanisches Englisch (BE) = britisches Englisch (v) = Verb, Zeitwort

A

a few ways einige Wege, *(hier)* einige Vorschläge 11/3A
a lot of viel, viele 2/1A
a piece of paper ein Blatt Papier 8E
A/C (air conditioning) Klimaanlage 9/2A
able to (to be ~) können, in der Lage sein, etwas zu tun 11/3A
Aboriginal der australischen Ureinwohner (Australiens) 9/Text
about über 5/2C; ungefähr, circa 9/1A
abroad Ausland 1/1B
accept (v) annehmen 14/2A
accommodate up to (v) Platz bieten für bis zu 9/2B
accommodation Unterkunft 2/1A
ache (v) schmerzen, weh tun 11/2A
activity Aktivität 8/B
add (v) hinzufügen 8/C
additional zusätzlich 9/2B
adult Erwachsene(r) 5/1B
advert Anzeige 9/2B
affected by (to be ~) von etwas betroffen sein 11/3A
afraid (I'm ~) ich fürchte 2/3A
again wieder 2/3A
agency Agentur 1/1A
ago vor 5/1B
agreeable angenehm 14/4A
air conditioning Klimaanlage 9/2A
all about alles über 7/5A
all in all alles in allem 10/2A
all inclusive alles inklusive 9/2C
alone allein 14/4A
along entlang 7/5A
along the way den Weg entlang 7/5A
although obwohl, obgleich 13/Text

always immer 3/2A
animal Tier 6/PSA
another eine andere, ein anderer / anderes 4/D
answer (v) antworten, beantworten 5/1D
answer the phone ans Telefon gehen 4/D
any irgendwelche 14/2C
Anything else? Sonst noch etwas?, Haben Sie noch einen Wunsch? 10/4A
appointment Termin 7/1B
appropriate geeignet, passend 11/1A
approximately ungefähr, circa 9/2B
area Bereich 9/2A; Region 15/3B
around um, herum 1/1A
arrive (v) ankommen 9/1A
artichoke Artischocke 10/3
artist Künstler 13/4A
as many as soviel wie 7/1B
as part of als Teil 13/4A
ask (v) fragen 5/1D
assistant (sales ~) Verkäufer/in 14/2A
associate (v) assoziieren 2/2A
at all (not ~) überhaupt nicht 13/4A
at first zuerst 5/1B
atmosphere Stimmung 10/1
available verfügbar 7/5A
average durchschnittlich 3/4A
avid begeistert, passioniert 7/5A
avoid (v) vermeiden 13/2

B

back Rücken 11/3C
back zurück 11/3C
bakery Bäckerei 6/1B
barbecue Grillfest 15/1A

basic einfach 3/3A
basil Basilikum 10/3
be (v) sein 1/1A
beach Strand 2/1A
beautiful schön 2/PSC
beauty product Schönheitsprodukt 14/Text
because weil 2/1D
become (v) werden 14/4A
bed and breakfast Übernachtung mit Frühstück 2/PSC
beef Rindfleisch 10/3
before vor, bevor 6/1B
below unten 14/1A
bike Fahrrad 6/1B
bill Rechnung 6/3A
black schwarz 14/2C
block of flats Wohnblock 13/PSE
blue blau 14/2C
board (on the ~) an der Tafel 2/2A
boarding pass Bordkarte 7/1C
boat trip Bootsausflug 9/1A
body Körper 11
book (v) buchen 7/1B
booking Buchung 9/2C
boots Stiefel 11/4B
boring langweilig 3/3A
born (be ~) (v) geboren werden 5/1B
bottle Flasche 15/1B
brainstorm (v) gemeinsam erarbeiten 6/1A
branch Zweigstelle 15/1B
break Pause 7/1A
break (v) brechen 11/2A
bridge Brücke 13/Text
bring a bottle bringt etwas zu trinken mit 15/1B
build (v) bauen 13/4A
building Gebäude 13/PSC
business Geschäft 5/1B
business meeting Geschäftsbesprechung 5/3

busy beschäftigt, voll 6/1B; besetzt 14/3C
buy *(v)* kaufen 5/1B
by bike mit dem Fahrrad 6/1B
by hand von Hand 6/1B
by the way übrigens 1/3A
by underground mit der U-Bahn 13/2

C

caffeine Koffein 11/3A
cage Käfig 14/1
call *(v)* anrufen 2/3A
caller Anrufer 2/3A
cancel *(v)* absagen 7/1B
capital Hauptstadt 10/Text
car rental Autovermietung 7/1B
cash Bargeld 14/1
casual clothes Freizeitkleidung 15/2A
catch *(v)* fangen 12/B
certainly aber natürlich, sicher 7/2A
chair Stuhl 9/2B
change Kleingeld 13/3A
change *(v)* umsteigen 13/2; verändern 13/4A
changes Veränderungen 13/4
chat *(v)* plaudern 14/4A
cheap billig 2/1A
check *(v)* prüfen 7/1B
checkout Kasse 14/3A
check-in Einchecken 7/1C
check-up Routineuntersuchung 7/2A
chef Koch, Köchin 3/1A
cheque Scheck 14/2A
chicken Huhn 10/3
choir Chor 3/1B
choose *(v)* wählen 12
city break Städtetour 7/1A
classifieds Kleinanzeigen 14/1
client Kunde, Kundin 6/3A
close *(v)* schließen 11/3C
clothes Kleidung 11/4B
cloudy wolkig, bewölkt 11/4A
coast Küste 7/5A
coat Mantel, Jacke 11/4B
coded verschlüsselt 4/C
coffee shop Café 13/4A
coffee table Couchtisch 14/3A
cold kalt 3/3A
colleague Kollege, Kollegin 13/PSB
collect *(v)* sammeln 1/2B; abholen 7/1B

college *(AE)* Universität, Fachhochschule 5/1B
come along *(v)* vorbeikommen 15/1B
comfortable bequem 2/1A
common health complaints häufige Gesundheits-beschwerden 11/2B
community beach Gemeindestrand 15/1B
commute *(v)* pendeln 14/4A
company Firma 1/1B
company Gesellschaft 15/1B
compare *(v)* vergleichen 3/4A
competition Wettbewerb 15/1B
complaint Beschwerde 11/2B
complete *(v)* vervollständigen 1/1B
contact *(v)* kontaktieren 6/2A
continue *(v)* weitermachen 12/E
convenient (to be ~) günstig sein 7/2A
conversation Gespräch 6/3A
convert into *(v)* sich umbauen lassen 9/2B
copy *(v)* kopieren 6/2A
costume Kostüm 15/1A
country (in the ~) auf dem Land 13/1A
countryside Landschaft 2/PSC
course Kurs 3/3B
create *(v)* machen, entwerfen 4/A
cross *(v)* überqueren 13/Text
cruise Kreuzfahrt 7/1A
cupboard Schrank 9/2A
cyber space Cyberspace 14/4A
cycle *(v)* Rad fahren 2/1A
cyclist Radfahrer 13/4A

D

daily newspaper Tageszeitung 3/2A
dairy product Milchprodukt 10/3A
dark dunkel 6/3A
daughter-in-law Schwiegertochter 1/1A
debit card Kundenkarte 13/3A
decode *(v)* entschlüsseln 4/C
delicious köstlich, sehr lecker 10/2A
deliver *(v)* liefern 14/4A
delivery Lieferung 10/1
delivery address Lieferadresse 14/3A

dental surgery Zahnarztpraxis 7/2A
dentist Zahnarzt, Zahnärztin 7/1B
department Abteilung 1/1A
describe *(v)* beschreiben 8/E
dessert Nachtisch, Dessert 10/3
destination (holiday ~) Urlaubsziel 2/1A
dialect Dialekt 6/Text
different verschieden 2/1A
dining area Essbereich 9/2A
dinner Abendessen 10/1A
dinner dance Abendessen mit Tanz 15/1A
directors (the ~) die Geschäftsführer 15/1B
discover *(v)* entdecken 13/2
dishwasher Spülmaschine 6/1A
do *(v)* tun, machen 6/1B
do sport *(v)* Sport treiben 11/3A
do yoga *(v)* Yoga machen 11/1D
document Dokument 6/2A
door Tür 14/4A
double bed Doppelbett 9/2B
down under *(informell)* Australien 9
draw *(v)* zeichnen, malen 8/E
dress Kleid 11/4B
drive *(v)* fahren 7/5A
driving licence Führerschein 9/3A
drop off someone / something jemanden absetzen, etwas abliefern 9/2B
dry trocken 11/4A

E

ear Ohr 11/PSG
easy leicht 13/2
economy (the ~) die Wirtschaft 15/3B
effective effektiv 5/3B
efficient effizient 5/3B
electricity Elektrizität, Strom 6/Text
emergency Notfall 6/3A
employee Angestellte/r 5/3B
enclose *(v)* beifügen 13/PSD
energy Energie, Kraft 11/3A
engineer Ingenieur/in 3/1A
enjoy *(v)* genießen 3/2A
enough genug 9/3A
equipment Ausstattung 9/2B
especially besonders 6/3A

essential notwendig 6/3A
evening suit Smoking 15/1A
everywhere überall 1/1B
except außer 14/4A
exception Ausnahme 3/Text
exchange (v) tauschen 4/C
excuse Entschuldigung 4/D
excuse me entschuldigen Sie 13/2D
exotic exotisch 10/1
expect (v) erwarten 5/3A
expensive teuer 3/3A
explain (v) erklären, erläutern 1/1B
export (v) exportieren 10/Text
expression Ausdruck 15/1B
eye Auge 11/3C

F

fact Tatsache, Fakt 5/2C
false falsch 3/4A
famous bekannt, berühmt 2/1A
fancy dress costume (Masken)kostüm 15/1A
fancy dress party Kostümparty 15/1A
farm Bauernhof 3/1A
farmhouse Bauernhaus 5/1B
favourite Lieblings~ 2/1C
fax machine Faxgerät 6/2A
feel (v) fühlen 11/2A
fewer weniger 3/4A
finally endlich 11/PSE
find out (v) herausfinden 5/2B
finger Finger 11/PSG
finish (v) fertig werden 5/1B
finish college (AE) Studium abschließen 5/1B
first of all zuerst 2/1A
fit in (v) (hier) einschieben 7/2A
flat Wohnung 5/1B
flight Flug 14/1A
flu (Abk. v. influenza) Grippe 11/2A
foggy neblig 11/4A
following (a survey) laut, nach einer Umfrage 2/1A
following (the ~) folgende 4/C
foot Fuß 11/3C
forget (v) vergessen 3/2A
form Formular 1/1C
formal formell 15/1B
freezer Gefrierschrank, Gefrierfach 9/2B
fridge Kühlschrank 9/2A
friends Freunde 14/4A
fruit Obst 10/3A

fully licensed mit Schankerlaubnis 10/1
future Zukunft 5/3C

G

game Spiel 14/4A
garlic Knoblauch 10/3
general information allgemeine Informationen 7/5A
get (v) bekommen 6/2A
get around (v) herumkommen 6/1B
get bigger (v) größer werden 6/3A
get off (v) aussteigen 13/2
get on (v) einsteigen 13/2
get on with someone (v) sich mit jemandem verstehen 5/3B
get things done (v) Dinge erledigen 14/4A
get to (v) erreichen 13/2
get to know (v) kennen lernen 1
give (v) geben 2/1D
give advice (v) Rat geben 7/5A
glass top Glasplatte 14/3B
gloves Handschuhe 11/4B
go on holiday (v) Urlaub machen 3/2A
go out (v) ausgehen 14/4A
go out for dinner essen gehen 10/1A
go shopping einkaufen gehen 3/2A
Good luck! Viel Glück! 15/3A
graduate (v) Studium abschließen 13/PSE
grandchildren Enkelkinder 1/1B
grandparents Großeltern 6/1A
great großartig 3/3
groceries Lebensmittel 14/1
grow vegetables Gemüse anbauen 6/1B
guaranteed garantiert 14/3A
guess (v) raten 8/B
gym Fitnessstudio 11/1A

H

half (the first ~) die erste Hälfte 8/B
ham Schinken 10/3
harbour Hafen 10/1
hard hart 3/4A
hate (v) hassen 14/4A
have (v) haben 6/1A

have a great time großartig gefallen 3/3
have a quiet / busy life ein ruhiges / arbeitsreiches Leben haben 6/1B
have breakfast (v) frühstücken 3/2A
have got (v) haben PS/14
have to (v) müssen 14/4A
have to do something (v) etwas machen müssen 7/1B
headache Kopfschmerzen 11/2A
health Gesundheit 11
healthy gesund 11/1C
heart Herz 13/2
help (v) helfen 11/3A
helpful hilfsbereit 3/3A
herbs Kräuter 10/3A
hermit Eremit 14/4A
high hoch 14/3A
high-tech lives Hightechleben 14/4
hike (v) wandern 2/1A
hill Hügel 13/1A
historical buildings historische Gebäude 13/PSC
history Geschichte 13/4A
hold (v) halten 4/D
hold (Would you like to ~?) Möchten Sie am Apparat bleiben? 14/3C
holiday Urlaub 2/1A
home office Büro zu Hause 14/4A
home town Heimatstadt 13/4C
hope (v) hoffen 13/4A
hopefully hoffentlich 15/3A
hour Stunde 3/4A
hourly wage Stundenlohn 3/4A
house-trained stubenrein 14/1
house-warming party Einweihungsfeier 15/1A
How about ...? Wie wär's mit ...? 10/1
how many wie viele 1/2B
however jedoch, dennoch 5/1B

I

if wenn, falls 11/4D
ill krank 11/2C
illness Krankheit 11/2B
imagine (v) sich etwas vorstellen 13/4C
important wichtig 1/1B
in (to be ~) zu Hause sein 2/3A
in a corner in einer Ecke 15/3A

in a hurry (to be ~) es eilig haben 14/4A
in any case jedenfalls 3/4A
in common gemeinsam 7/3B
in fact in der Tat 11/2A
in those days damals 6/2B
in total insgesamt 9/PSF
include *(v)* einschließen 9/2B
including einschließlich 3/4A
income Einkommen 3/4A
independent unabhängig 5/3B
indoor swimming pool Hallenbad 13/PSC
industrial area Industriegebiet 13/PSC
informal informell 15/1B
inside innen 10/1
instead anstatt, anstelle 9/PSA
internet user Internetnutzer 14/Text
interview someone *(v)* jemanden interviewen 3/2B
introduce oneself *(v)* sich vorstellen 1/1D
invitation Einladung 15/1A
invite *(v)* einladen 15/1B
item Artikel 14/1A

K

keep fit *(v)* sich fit halten 11/1C
keep the conversation going *(v)* das Gespräch in Gang halten 16/C
kind of (a ~) Art 7/5A
kind of you (it was very ~) es war sehr nett von Ihnen 15/4A
kinds (all ~ of) allerlei 14/4A
kitchen Küche 9/2A
kiwi(fruit) Kiwi 10/3
knee Knie 11/PSG

L

label *(v)* bezeichnen 1/2A
large groß 9/2B
last night letzte Nacht 6/3A
late spät, zu spät 5/3B
late (be ~) *(v)* zu spät sein 5/3B
latest neueste 15/3B
leave *(v)* abgeben 9/1A
leave *(v)* liegen lassen 13/3A
leave a message *(v)* eine Nachricht hinterlassen 2/3A
leave school *(v)* die Schule abschließen 6/2A

leaving party Abschiedsfeier 15/1A
left links 16/C
leg Bein 11/3C
less weniger 3/4A
let *(v)* lassen 15/1B
letter Buchstabe 4/A
letter Brief 15/4A
licensed (fully ~) mit Schankerlaubnis 10/1
life (it's a hard ~) das Leben ist hart 3/4A
lift *(v)* heben 11/3C
light (in a new ~) in einem neuen Licht 13/2
like mögen 2/3A
like (I'd ~) ich möchte 2/3A
like (What's she ~?) Wie ist sie? 15/3B
limit oneself *(v)* sich beschränken 14/4A
line is busy (the ~) die Leitung ist besetzt 14/3C
living area Wohnbereich 9/2A
local einheimisch 9/Text
locate *(v)* ausfindig machen 13/2A
look after *(v)* jemanden pflegen, sich um jemanden kümmern 3/1B
look at *(v)* anschauen, besichtigen 1/1B
look back *(v)* zurückblicken 5
look for *(v)* suchen 6/3A
look for jobs Stellen / Jobs suchen 14/4A
look forward to *(v)* sich auf etwas freuen 3/3B
look like *(v)* aussehen wie 13/Text
look through *(v)* durchsehen 5/3A
lost property office Fundbüro 13/3A
lovely schön 10/2A
low niedrig 14/1
luxurious luxuriös 3/3A

M

made of aus 14/3A
main course Hauptgericht 10/3
mainly hauptsächlich 6/Text
make *(v)* machen 6/3A
make *(v)* backen 6/1B
make a reservation *(v)* eine Reservierung vornehmen 14/Text

make appointments *(v)* Termine ausmachen 6/3B
make calls *(v)* Telefongespräche führen 6/4
make friends *(v)* Freunde finden 14/4A
make payable to *(v)* auf jemanden ausstellen 14/1
make sure *(v)* darauf achten 9/3A
managing director Geschäftsführer 15/3B
map Landkarte 9/1A
married verheiratet 1/Text
match *(v)* zuordnen 1/QQ
meal Mahlzeit 15/2A
means of transport Beförderungsmittel 9/1B
meat Fleisch 10/3A
meet *(v)* treffen, kennen lernen 1/1D
menu Speisekarte 10/3
message Nachricht 2/3A
metal base Metallfuß 14/3A
microwave Mikrowelle 9/2A
mileage Meilenstand 14/1
mime *(v)* pantomimisch darstellen 8/B
miss *(v)* vermissen 5/1B
more and more often immer häufiger 1/Text
most (the ~) der / die / das meiste 3/4A
most of all am meisten 5/1B
motorhome Wohnmobil 7/5A
mountain Berg 13/1A
move *(v)* umziehen 5/1A
move to *(v)* nach ... ziehen 5/1A
move up *(v)* hochklappen 13/Text
movement Bewegung 5/1A
mushroom Champignon 10/3
mussels Muscheln 10/3

N

National Tourist Board Nationaler Tourismusverband 2/1A
native speaker Muttersprachler/in 3/Text
nearly fast 6/Text
neck Hals 11/PSG
need *(v)* brauchen 1
neighbour Nachbar/in 12/E
Neither do I. Ich auch nicht. 7/1A

never nie 3/2A
newspaper Zeitung 2/1A
next to neben 7/1B
nice schön, nett 1/1D
no longer nicht mehr 14/4A
normally normalerweise 11/4B
nose Nase 11/2A
not just nicht nur 2/1A
note *(v)* notieren 7/3A
nowadays heutzutage 6/2B
number *(v)* nummerieren 6/2A

O

of course natürlich 2/3C
office Büro 3/1A
official Sprecher, Beamte 2/1A
often oft, häufig 1/1A
old-fashioned altmodisch 6/Text
on my own allein 15/3A
on your right / left zu Ihrer Rechten / Linken 16/C
once einmal 11/1C
onion Zwiebel 10/3
online online 14/Text
only nur 1/Text
opening Eröffnung 15/1B
opera Oper 9/1A
order (in the ~) in der Reihenfolge 3/1B
order *(v)* bestellen 10/4A
order form Bestellformular 14/3A
organize *(v)* organisieren 7/1B
outfit Kleidung 15/2A
outside draußen 10/1
over über 13/4A
overlook *(v)* überblicken 10/1

P

P + R (Abk. v. Park and Ride) Park-and-ride-System 13/2
pack *(v)* packen 7/1C
part Teil 13/4A
pass *(v)* weitergeben 12/E
pass under *(v)* unter durch-fahren 13/Text
passenger ticket Fluggastticket 7/1C
path Weg 13/4A
pay *(v)* bezahlen 14/1B
payable zahlbar 14/1
per pro 3/4A

performance Leistung 5/3A
performance review Beurteilung 5/3A
personal details Personalien 9/2B
pet Haustier 14/1
petrol Benzin 9/3A
phone conversation Telefongespräch 6/3A
photocopier Fotokopierer 6/2A
physically active (to be ~) körperlich aktiv sein 11/3A
piano Klavier 3/1B
pick up someone / something *(v)* jemanden / etwas abholen 9/2B
picture Gemälde 13/4A
play *(v)* spielen 2/1A
pleasure Vergnügen 15/1B
plenty of viel 9/2B
poor schlecht 10/2B
popular beliebt 2/1A
possible möglich 7/1B
potato Kartoffel 10/3
practise *(v)* üben 2/3D
prawns Garnelen 10/3
prefer *(v)* bevorzugen 7/1A
present *(v)* vorstellen 5/2C
produce *(v)* produzieren 10/Text
product Produkt 10/3A
productive produktiv 5/3B
pronunciation Aussprache 2/3D
public holiday Feiertag 3/4A
public place öffentlicher Ort 6/3A
pull *(v)* ziehen 11/3C
pullover Pullover 14/PSF
punctual pünktlich 5/3B
purchase *(v)* kaufen, erwerben 14/1
purchasing Einkauf 5/3B
purse Portemonnaie 13/3A

Q

quality Qualität 14/3A
quantity Quantität 14/3A
questionnaire Fragebogen 3/2A
quickly (as ~ as possible) so schnell wie möglich 16/B
quiet ruhig 6/1B
quite ziemlich 13/1B

R

R.S.V.P. um Antwort wird gebeten 15/1B
rafting Rafting 2/1A
railway Eisenbahn 9/1A
rainy regnerisch 3/3B
raise *(v)* heben 11/3C
read along lesen Sie mit 16/D
reader Leser/in 2/1A
really wirklich 3/3B
reason Grund 1/1C
receipt Kassenzettel, Quittung 14/2C
recently neulich 10/2C
recommend *(v)* empfehlen 9/2B
reduce *(v)* reduzieren, abbauen 11/3A
regards Gruß 3/3B
regularly regelmäßig 11/1B
relaxation Entspannung 11/3A
relaxed dining Speisen in entspannter Atmosphäre 10/1
religious community religiöse Gemeinschaft 6/Text
remedy Heilmittel 11/2C
removal Entfernung, Abnahme 5/1A
remove *(v)* entfernen, beseitigen, abnehmen 5/1A
renovate *(v)* renovieren 5/1B
repeat *(v)* wiederholen 11/3C
reply Antwort 4/C
reply *(v)* beantworten 15/1B
report *(v)* berichten 2/1A
request *(v)* um etwas bitten 15/1B
required erforderlich 7/1B
right rechts 16/C
river Fluss 13/1A
road Straße 7/5A
road atlas Straßenatlas 9/2B
road trip *Tour per Auto oder Wohnmobil durch ein Land/eine Region* 7/5A
roof Dach 13/4A
round rund 14/3A
route Strecke 7/5A
rule Regel 12/D
run a business *(v)* ein Geschäft betreiben 5/1B

S

safe sicher 6/3A
salary Gehalt 15/3B

sales Vertrieb 5/3B
sales assistant Verkäufer/in 14/2A
salmon Lachs 10/3
same (the ~) der/die/dasselbe 6/Text
sandcastle competition Sandburgenwettbewerb 15/1B
satisfaction is guaranteed (your ~) Ihre Zufriedenheit wird garantiert 14/3A
sauce Soße 10/3
save (v) sparen 6/3A
scarf Schal 11/4B
sea Meer 13/1A
seafood Meeresfrüchte 10/1
season Jahreszeit 11/4A
seat belt Sicherheitsgurt 9/3A
second-hand gebraucht 14/1A
security Sicherheit 14/Text
see you bis dann 1/3A
send (v) schicken, verschicken 6/3B
service Bedienung 10/2A
shall (we ~ see) wir werden sehen 15/4A
shelter Unterstand 6/4
ship Schiff 13/Text
shop (v) einkaufen 14/1A
shoulder Schulter 11/PSG
shoulder blade Schulterblatt 11/3C
show around (v) herumführen 1/1A
shower Dusche 9/2A
showers Regenschauer 11/4A
shrimps Schrimps 10/3
side Seite 16/D
side salad Salatbeilage 10/3
sightsee (v) besichtigen 9/1A
sign (v) unterschreiben 14/2A
simple einfach 12/C
since seit 13/4A
sit (v) sitzen 15/3A
skirt Rock 11/4B
skunk Stinktier 14/1
slow langsam 5/3B
small talk Smalltalk, oberflächliche Konversation 15/3A
smile (v) lächeln 7/3
snack kleiner Imbiss 15/2A
snow Schnee 11/4A
So do I. Ich auch. 2/1D
socialise (v) sich unterhalten 15/3A
some einige 14/2C

someone else jemand anders 12/B
sometimes manchmal 1/1B
soon bald 5/1B
sore throat Halsschmerzen 11/2A
soul Seele 11/1
soup Suppe 10/3
spacious geräumig 9/2B
spell (v) buchstabieren 2/2A
spelling Schreibweise 2/3D
spend time (v) Zeit verbringen 14/4A
spices Gewürze 10/3A
spicy würzig 10/3
standard Standard, Qualitätsstufe 14/3A
standard equipment Standardausstattung 9/2B
start (v) anfangen 5/1B
starter Vorspeise 10/3
statement Aussage 6/2B
statistic Statistik 3/4A
stay (v) (hier) übernachten 3/3B
steal (v) stehlen 13/3A
step Stufe 9/2A
stick (v) kleben 12/C
sticky klebrig 10/4B
still noch 6/2A
storage space Stauraum 9/2B
store card Kundenkarte 14/2A
story Geschichte 5/2
stove Herd 9/2A
straight gerade 11/3C
stretch (v) strecken 11/3C
stylish stilvoll 14/3A
suddenly plötzlich 6/3A
suitcase Koffer 7/1B
sun cream Sonnenschutzcreme 7/1B
sunshine Sonnenschein 11/4C
surname Nachname, Familienname 1/1C
survey Umfrage 2/1A
sweet süß 10/3
sweets Süßigkeiten, Bonbons 11/2C
swimming costume Badeanzug 15/1A
swimming pool Schwimmbad 13/PSC
syllable Silbe 2/1B

T

table Tisch 9/2A
take (v) nehmen 5/3A

take a boat trip (v) einen Bootsausflug machen 9/1A
take a photo (v) ein Foto machen 6/3B
take a seat? (Why don't you ~) Warum nehmen Sie nicht Platz? 5/3A
take home (v) mit nach Hause nehmen 10/1A
takeaway Gericht zum Mitnehmen 10/1
task Aufgabe 5/3B
taste Geschmack 10/1
tasteless wenig schmackhaft, fade 10/2B
technique Methode, Technik 11/3A
tell (v) erzählen 3/2C
terrible schrecklich 3/3A
text message SMS 6/3B
thank-you letter Dankesbrief 15/4A
think (v) finden 6/3C
think carefully about (v) gründlich darüber nachdenken 5/3C
think of (v) sich ausdenken 4/B
three quarters drei viertel 14/Text
three times dreimal 11/1C
through (I'll put you ~) ich verbinde Sie, ich stelle Sie durch 14/3B
throw (v) werfen 4/D
thunderstorm Gewitter 11/4A
ticket machine Fahrkartenautomat 13/3A
tie Krawatte 15/1A
time Zeit 6/3A
timeline Zeitlinie 5/1C
today heute 7/3A
toe Zeh 11/3C
together zusammen 11/3C
top quality Spitzenqualität 14/3A
topic Thema 15/3A
towards Richtung 13/2C
traffic jam Verkehrsstau 13/2
training course Ausbildungskurs 3/3B
translate (v) übersetzen 8/E
transport Verkehrsmittel 9/1B
travel (v) reisen 1/1B
travel agency Reisebüro 1/1A
travel agent Reisebürokaufmann/frau 7/1B

travelling Reisen 1/1A
trip Reise, Ausflug 9
true richtig, wahr 3/4A
try *(v)* ausprobieren 11/3A
try *(v)* versuchen 8/C
try on *(v)* anprobieren 14/Text
tube (the ~) die Londoner
U-Bahn 13/2
turn off *(v)* ausschalten 6/3A
twice zweimal 11/1C
two thirds zwei drittel
14/Text

U

umbrella Regenschirm 13/3A
unbelievable unglaublich
6/3A
under unter 1/1A
underline *(v)* unterstreichen
5/1B
unemployed arbeitslos 1/1A
until bis 4/D
use *(v)* verwenden 14/3A
usually normalerweise 3/2A

V

valid gültig 9/3A

vegetables Gemüse 6/1B
vegetarian vegetarisch,
Vegetarier/in 10/3
very sehr 3/3B
vet (Abk. v. veterinarian)
Tierarzt, Tierärztin 3/1A
village Dorf 13/1A
vineyard Weingut 10/Text

W

wage Lohn 3/4A
wait in a queue *(v)* Schlange
stehen 14/4A
walk *(v)* zu Fuß gehen 6/Text
walker Wanderer 13/4A
wardrobe Kleiderschrank
9/2A
wash basin Waschbecken
9/2A
watch out *(v)* sich in Acht
nehmen 9/3A
way Weg 7/5A
way of life Lebensweise
6/Text
wear *(v)* tragen 15/1A
wear a seat belt *(v)*
angeschnallt sein 9/3A
weather Wetter 11/4

wedding Hochzeit 15/1C
weekly wöchentlich 11/4C
welcome (you're ~) gern
geschehen, bitte 7/2A
whatever ganz gleich 11/4
while während 5/3A
while (for a ~) für eine Weile
16/C
whole ganz 11/2A
why warum 5/3A
window Fenster 13/1D
wishes (best ~) beste
Wünsche 15/4A
without ohne 10/4A
wonderful wunderbar 15/3B
work Arbeit 3/2A
work *(v)* arbeiten 1/1A
working hours Arbeitsstunden
3/4A
worldwide weltweit 14/Text
worry Sorge 14/4A
worry about *(v)* sich Sorgen
machen über 14/Text
wrap *(v)* einpacken 14/2A

Y

yesterday gestern 6/3A

Quellenverzeichnis

S. 8 und 9: 1. Getty Images (EyeWire), München; 2. IBM Deutschland GmbH, Stuttgart; 3. Getty Images (EyeWire), München; 4. Getty Images (PhotoDisc), München; 5. Getty Images (PhotoDisc), München; **S. 10:** Elmar Feuerbach, Remshalden; **S. 11:** Elmar Feuerbach, Remshalden; **S. 16:** 1. Getty Images (EyeWire), München; 2. IBM Deutschland GmbH, Stuttgart; 3. Getty Images (EyeWire), München; 4. Getty Images (PhotoDisc), München; 5. Getty Images (PhotoDisc), München; **S. 18:** Comma Pictures, Helsinki; **S. 20:** (oben) MEV, Augsburg; (unten – links) MEV, Augsburg; (unten – rechts) Getty Images (PhotoDisc), München; **S. 21:** Comma Pictures, Helsinki; **S. 22:** Siemens AG, München; **S. 25:** (oben) Corbis Digital Stock, London; (unten) MEV, Augsburg; **S. 28:** 1. – 3. Getty Images (PhotoDisc), München; 4. IBM Deutschland GmbH, Stuttgart; 5. und 6. Getty Images (PhotoDisc), München; **S. 30:** Corbis Digital Stock, London; **S. 34:** 1. und 2. Corbis Digital Stock, London; 3. Getty Images, München; 4. und 5. Corbis Digital Stock, London; **S. 38:** (links) Corbis UK Limited, London; (rechts) MEV, Augsburg; **S. 40:** (oben) Corbis Digital Stock, London; (unten) Getty Images (EyeWire), München; **S. 41:** (links) Getty Images (EyeWire), München; (rechts) Corbis Digital Stock, London; (Mitte – rechts) Air Canada, Dorval; **S. 43:** PhotoAlto (Eric Audras), Paris; **S. 44:** IBM Deutschland GmbH, Stuttgart; **S. 47:** Corbis Digital Stock, London; **S. 48:** Getty Images (PhotoDisc), München; **S. 50:** (oben – links) Robert Bosch GmbH, Stuttgart; (oben – rechts) ALNO AG, Pfullendorf; (Mitte – links) Hewlett-Packard, Böblingen; (Mitte) Miele, Gütersloh; (Mitte – rechts) Siemens AG, München; (unten – rechts) Citroen Deutschland AG, Köln; **S. 51:** Getty Images (PhotoDisc), München; **S. 52:** IBM Deutschland GmbH, Stuttgart; **S. 53:** (oben – links) MEV, Augsburg; (rechts) Getty Images (EyeWire), München; (links) MEV, Augsburg; (unten – rechts) Getty Images (EyeWire), München; **S. 54:** The Spectator Limited, London; **S. 56:** (links) www.britainonview.com, London; (rechts) Corbis Digital Stock, London; **S. 60:** (links – rechts) MEV, Augsburg; MEV, Augsburg; (oben – rechts) Getty Images (EyeWire), München; (rechts) Getty Images (EyeWire), München; **S. 61:** (links) IBM Deutschland GmbH, Stuttgart; (Mitte) Nicola Tuson, Stuttgart; (rechts) PhotoAlto, Paris; **S. 62:** Getty Images (EyeWire), München; **S. 63:** Getty Images (PhotoDisc), München; **S. 64:** James Oehmke, Stuttgart; **S. 69:** (links) Corbis Digital Stock, London; (rechts) Getty Images, München; **S. 70:** MEV, Augsburg; **S. 71:** (links) Getty Images (PhotoDisc), Hamburg; (Mitte) Siemens AG, München; (rechts) BMW AG, München; **S. 72:** (links) Getty Images, München; (Mitte) MEV, Augsburg; (Mitte – unten) Great Southern Railways, Marleston, South Australia; (oben – rechts) MEV, Augsburg; **S. 74:** (oben) Great Southern Railways, Marleston, South Australia; (Mitte und unten) Apollo Motorhome Holidays Pty Ltd, Northgate (Brisbane), Australia; **S. 75:** Apollo Motorhome Holidays Pty Ltd, Northgate (Brisbane), Australia; **S. 76:** Getty Images, München; **S. 78:** (oben) MEV, Augsburg; (unten) Getty Images (PhotoDisc), München; **S. 79:** Corbis Digital Stock, London; **S. 80:** (links) Airbus SAS, Blagnac; (rechts) Getty Images (PhotoDisc), München; **S. 81:** Getty Images (PhotoDisc), München; **S. 82:** MEV, Augsburg; **S. 85:** Gilbert van Reenen; **S. 86:** (oben) Corbis Digital Stock, London; (unten) The Spectator Limited, London; **S. 89:** The Spectator Limited, London; **S. 92:** (links) Getty Images (EyeWire), München; (oben – links) MEV, Augsburg; (oben – Mitte) MEV, Augsburg; (oben – rechts) Corbis Digital Stock, London; (Mitte – unten) Corbis Digital Stock, London; (unten – rechts) Getty Images (EyeWire), München; **S. 95:** MEV, Augsburg; **S. 101:** Getty Images (EyeWire), München; **S. 104:** (oben – links) James Oehmke, Stuttgart; (oben – rechts) Corbis Digital Stock, London; (unten – links) www.britainonview.com, London; (unten – rechts) Corbis Digital Stock, London; **S. 105:** (oben) Joachim Krüger, Stuttgart; (unten) Corbis Digital Stock, London; **S. 106:** (links) Getty Images, München; (Mitte) Getty Images (PhotoDisc), Hamburg; (rechts) David Shallis, Weil der Stadt; **S. 108:** (links) www.britainonview.com, London; (rechts) Klett-Archiv, Stuttgart; (unten) Graeme Peacock, Newcastle upon Tyne; **S. 110:** (links) Getty Images (PhotoDisc), München; (rechts) MEV, Augsburg; **S. 112:** (links) Getty Images (EyeWire), München; (rechts) Klett – Archiv, Stuttgart; **S. 114:** (links) Elmar Feuerbach, Remshalden; (Mitte) Europäische Zentralbank, Frankfurt; (oben – rechts) Elmar Feuerbach, Remshalden; **S. 116:** (links) Team 7, Ried; (rechts) Ronald Schmitt Tische GmbH, Eberbach; **S. 117:** Corbis Digital Stock, London; **S. 118:** Getty Images (EyeWire), München; **S. 121:** (links) Ronald Schmitt Tische GmbH, Eberbach; (rechts) Team 7, Ried; **S. 124:** (oben – links) MEV, Augsburg; (oben – rechts) Getty Images (PhotoDisc), München; (unten – links) Corbis Digital Stock, London; (unten – rechts) Getty Images (PhotoDisc), München; **S. 126:** Corbis Digital Stock (RF), London; **S. 127:** Getty Images (EyeWire), München; **S. 131:** Corbis Digital Stock, London; **S. 132:** Creativ Collection Verlag GmbH, Freiburg; **S. 134:** MEV, Augsburg

In einigen Fällen ist es uns trotz intensiver Bemühungen nicht gelungen, die Rechte-Inhaber zu ermitteln. Wir bitten diese, sich mit dem Verlag in Verbindung zu setzen.

Alle Firmennamen sind frei erfunden.